HERE'S YOUR DAMNED COLORING BOOK

by James "Trey" Howell

Text and image copyright 2017 by James "Trey" Howell

For Dad

Other works by James "Trey" Howell

The Man and the Moon

The Station Heist

Fury of the Mistress, Part One

Fury of the Mistress, Part Two (*maybe, eventually*)

INTRODUCTION

I ain't no rocket scientist, as I continually prove to myself and everyone else, but my dad is a mechanical engineer who helped to put a man on the Moon. Or rather, he was. A few months back he had a stroke and now he is a mischievous, damaged person with very busy hands. He needs a coloring book, and honestly, I don't have the time or the energy to work on my own science fiction series right now, anyway. But I still haven't forgotten how to crap out a book.

I also happen to know that nobody ever reads these introductions, nobody buys adult coloring books anymore, and nobody at all buys adult coloring books that aren't promoted except with maybe a side mention on Facebook, where nobody sees that they can buy all my other books, which they don't want anyway.

So here's some big fat stinky wads of cow poop to all of you nobodies out there. I don't give a damn what you think, even if you are a *somebody* who actually bought this, and if you don't like this book you can roll it up and shove it straight up your arse. Hey, this is an adult coloring book; I can say what I want.

Here's your damned coloring book, Dad. I love you very much.

– Trey, September, 2017

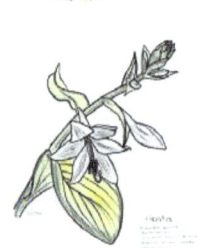
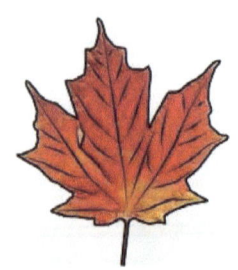
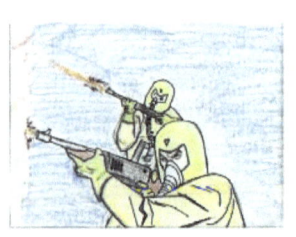
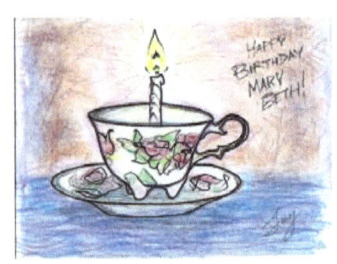
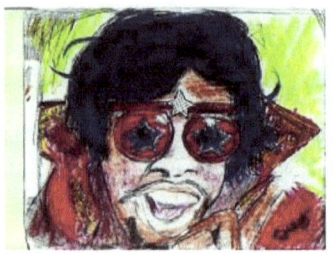
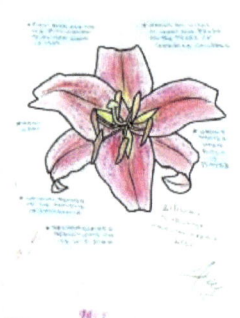
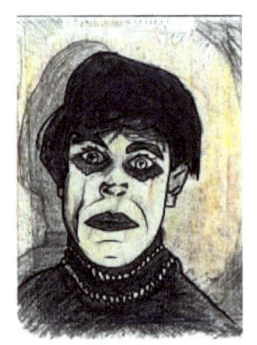
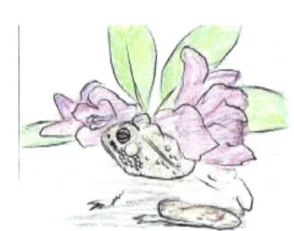
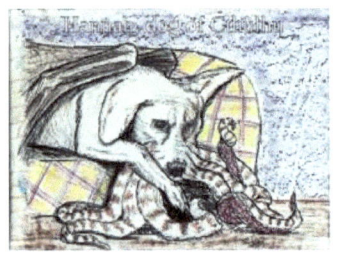
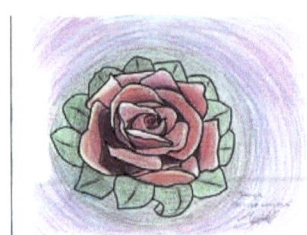
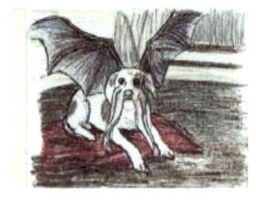
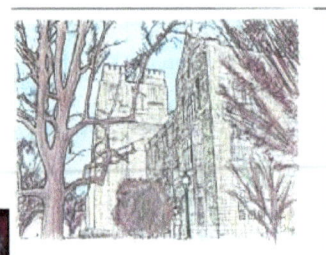
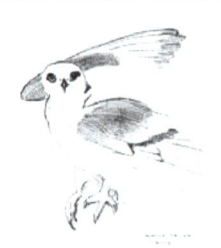
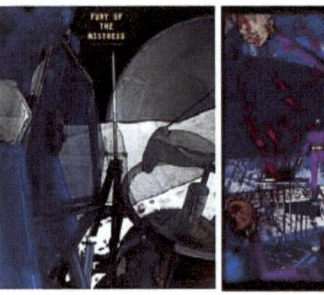
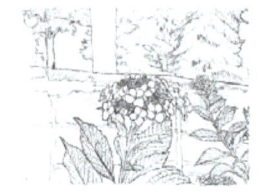
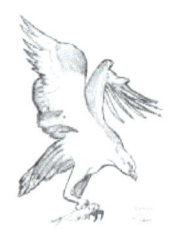
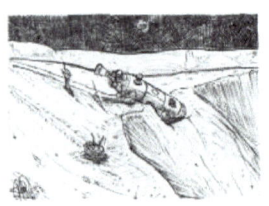

PART ONE: COLOR ALONG WITH TREY

Some of these images were drawn on the spot from real life. Others are not. Still others are low-down dirty tricks where I simply traced lines over a photograph, or used other artifice. That's why I call myself a fake artist, and if you don't like it, I suggest that you start reading the introductions to books. Anyway, you've got my attempt on the left side, which you are free to duplicate or ignore as you see fit, and a line drawing on the right, which is where you come in. Part Three is a "Do Over" section, so if you screw it up you have a second or maybe even third chance, depending on how well the various programs that put all this crap together hold up. Maybe I'll edit this part, too, but probably not.

Pro tip on coloring: Start with your lightest, brightest colors first. Crayons in particular don't like to draw on top of other layers of crayon, so you can use white as a "do not accidentally draw here" barrier. But it doesn't always work. Also, you can save yourself some heartbreak by testing the crayons you want to use on the margins of the page, to make sure they're the ones you want—you can see me doing that in some of the images in the pages beyond. If you're a perfectionist, well, you've come to the wrong place, first of all, but you might take the giant leap of testing your crayons on another page, like this one, if you really don't want to screw up your picture. If you're that person, you surely also have an X-acto knife and a ruler so that you can carefully cut the pages out. You probably also fold your underwear… don't you?

That's about all I've got in the talent bag, as you'll soon see. Oh, wait--try not to drool on the page, as I sometimes do.

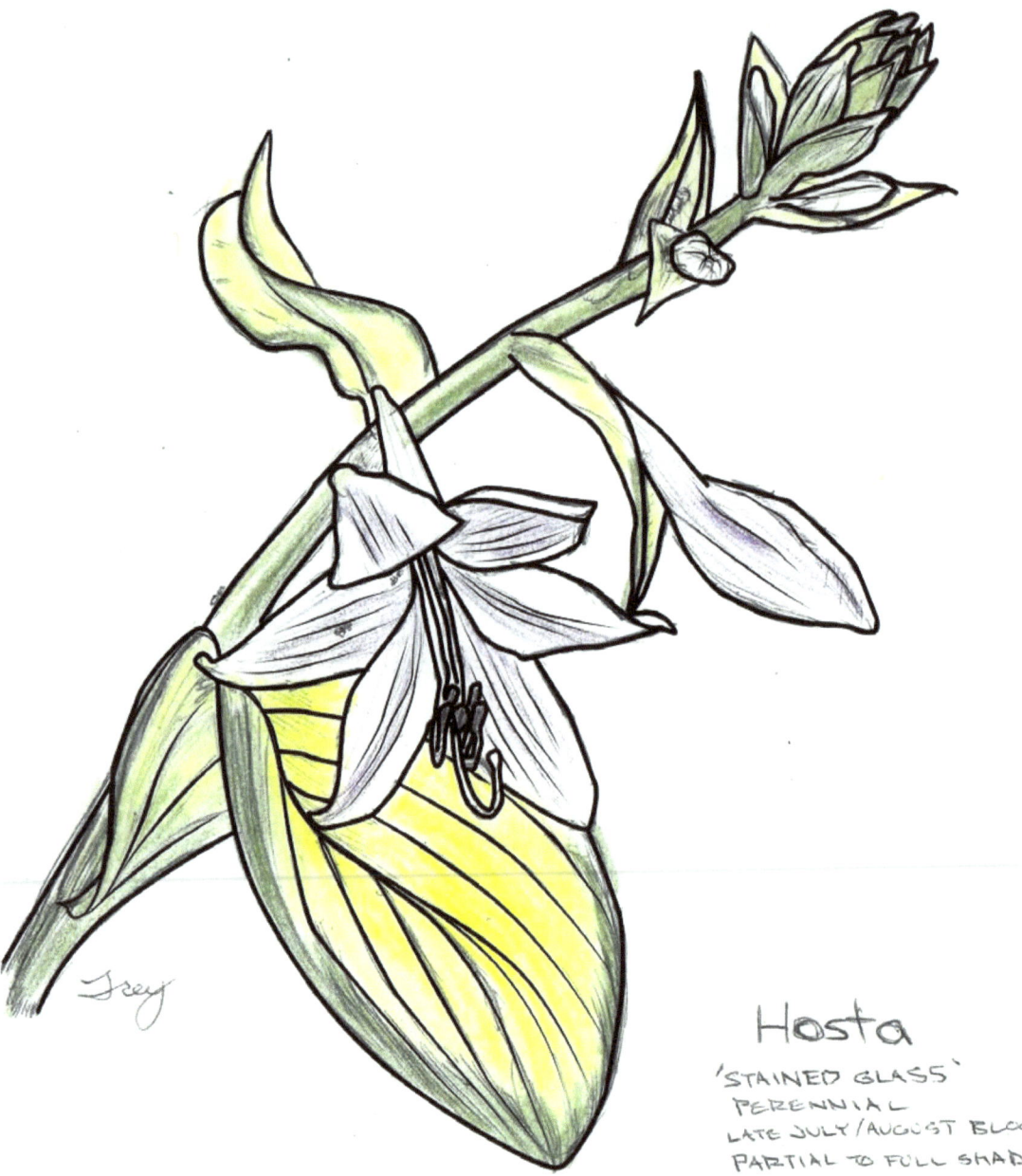

Hosta
'STAINED GLASS'
PERENNIAL
LATE JULY/AUGUST BLOOM
PARTIAL TO FULL SHADE
MOIST SOIL
24" (61CM) TALL

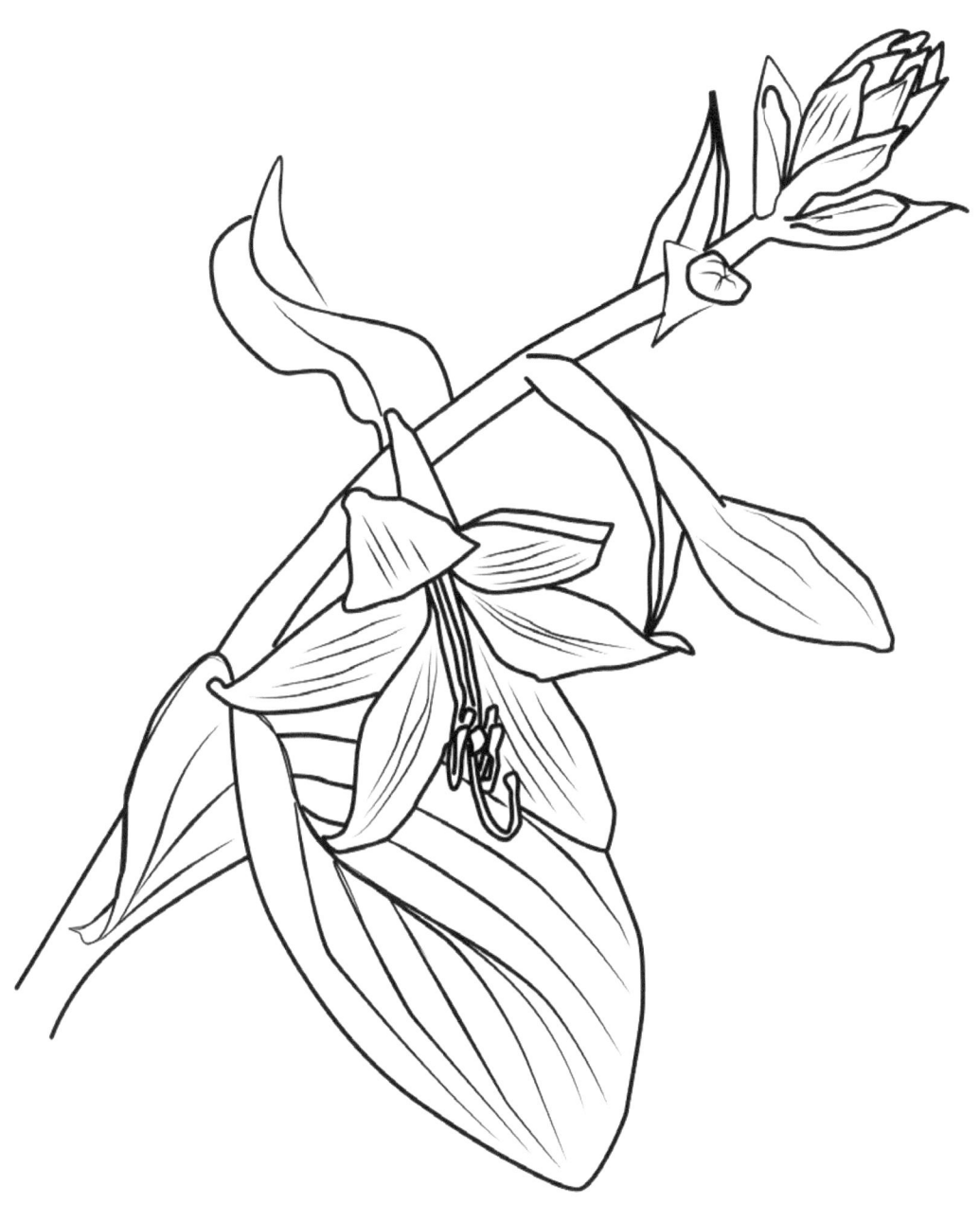

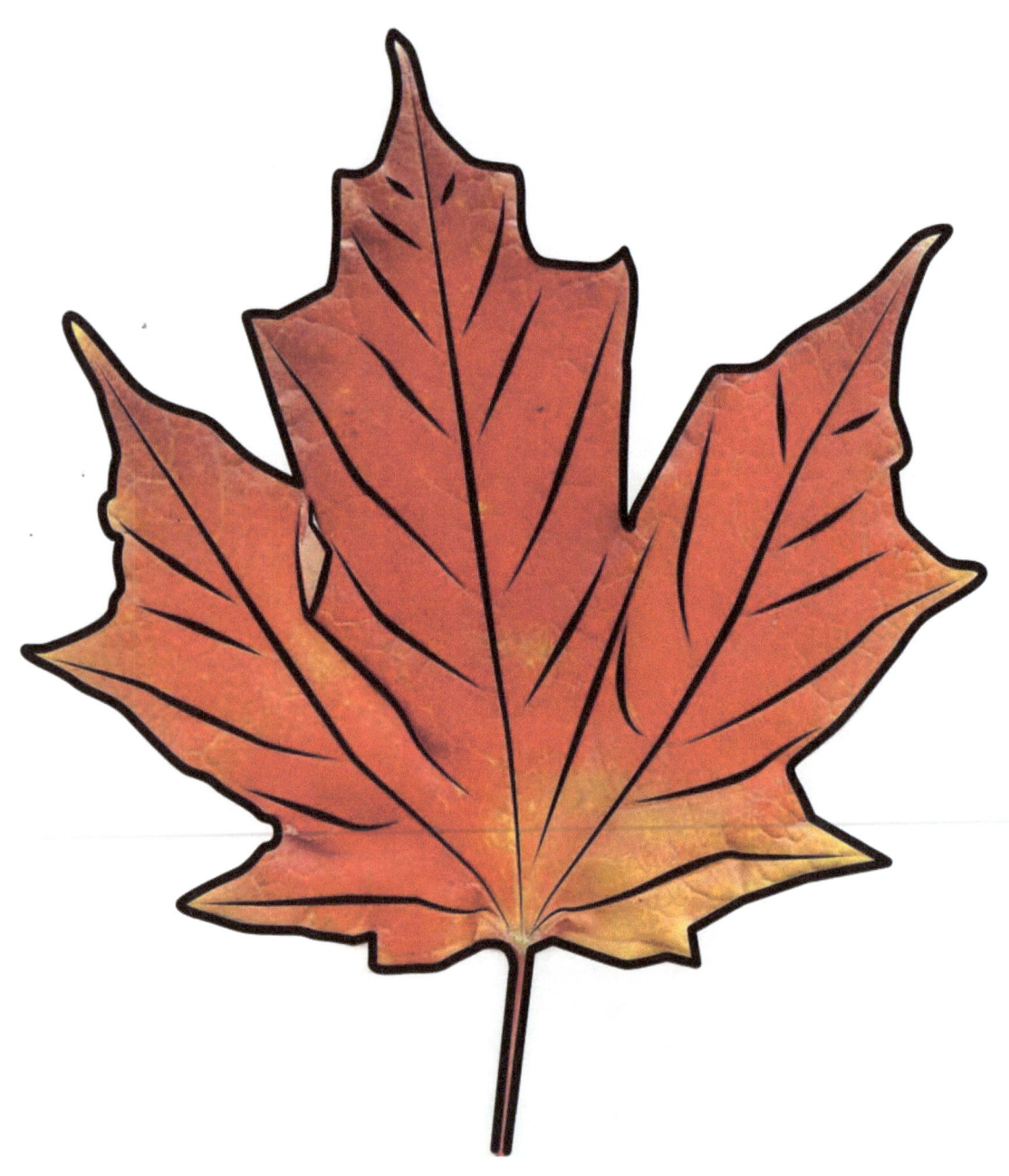

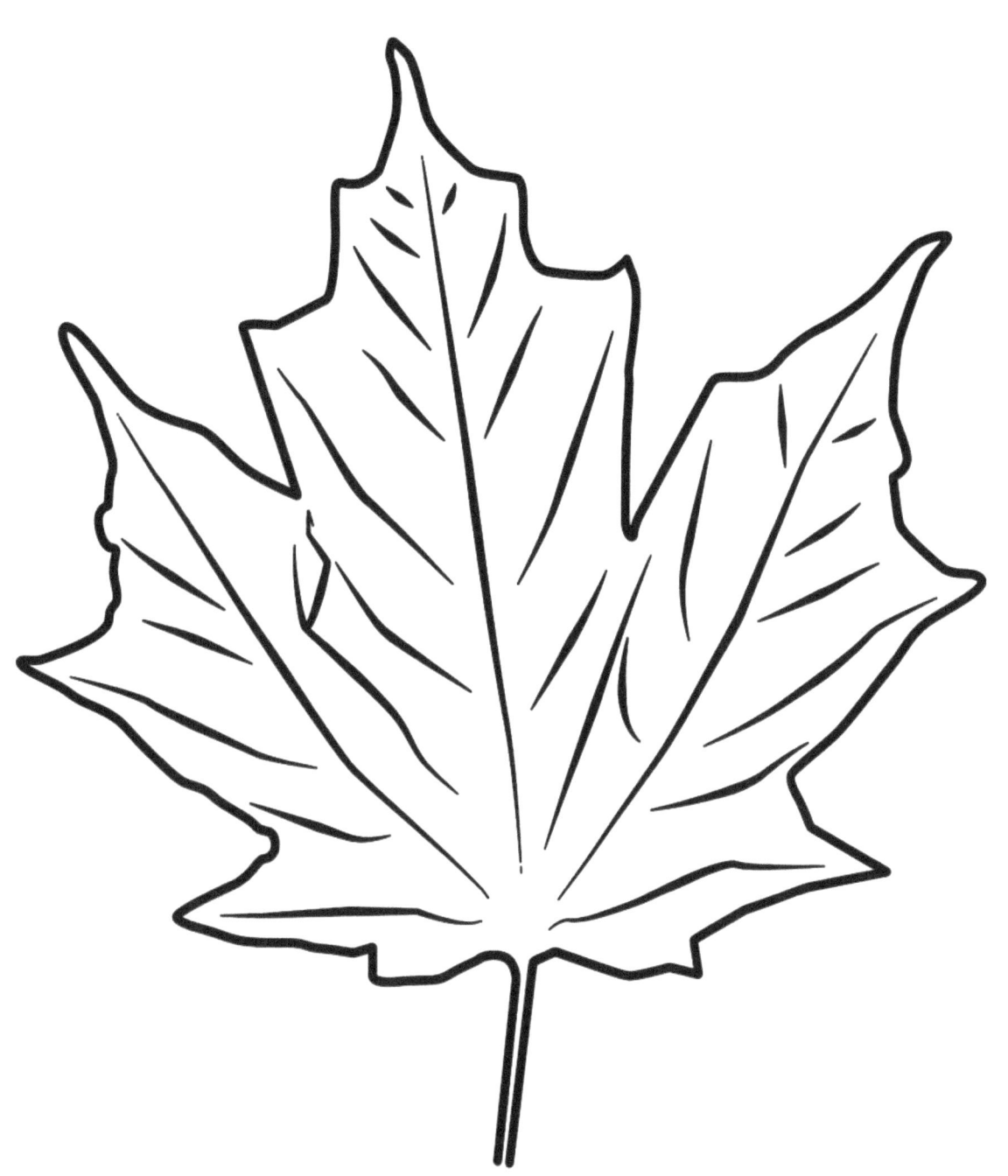

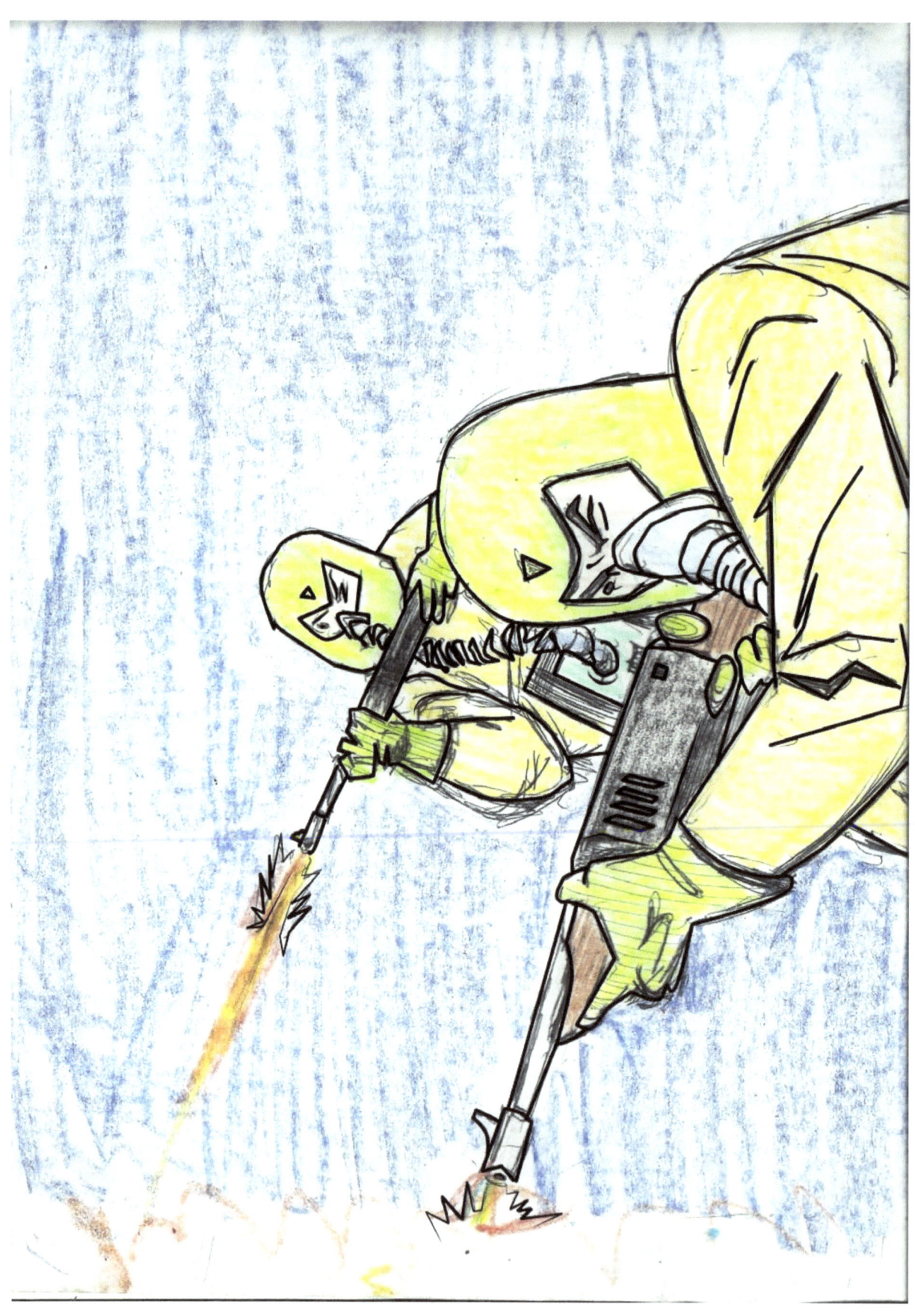

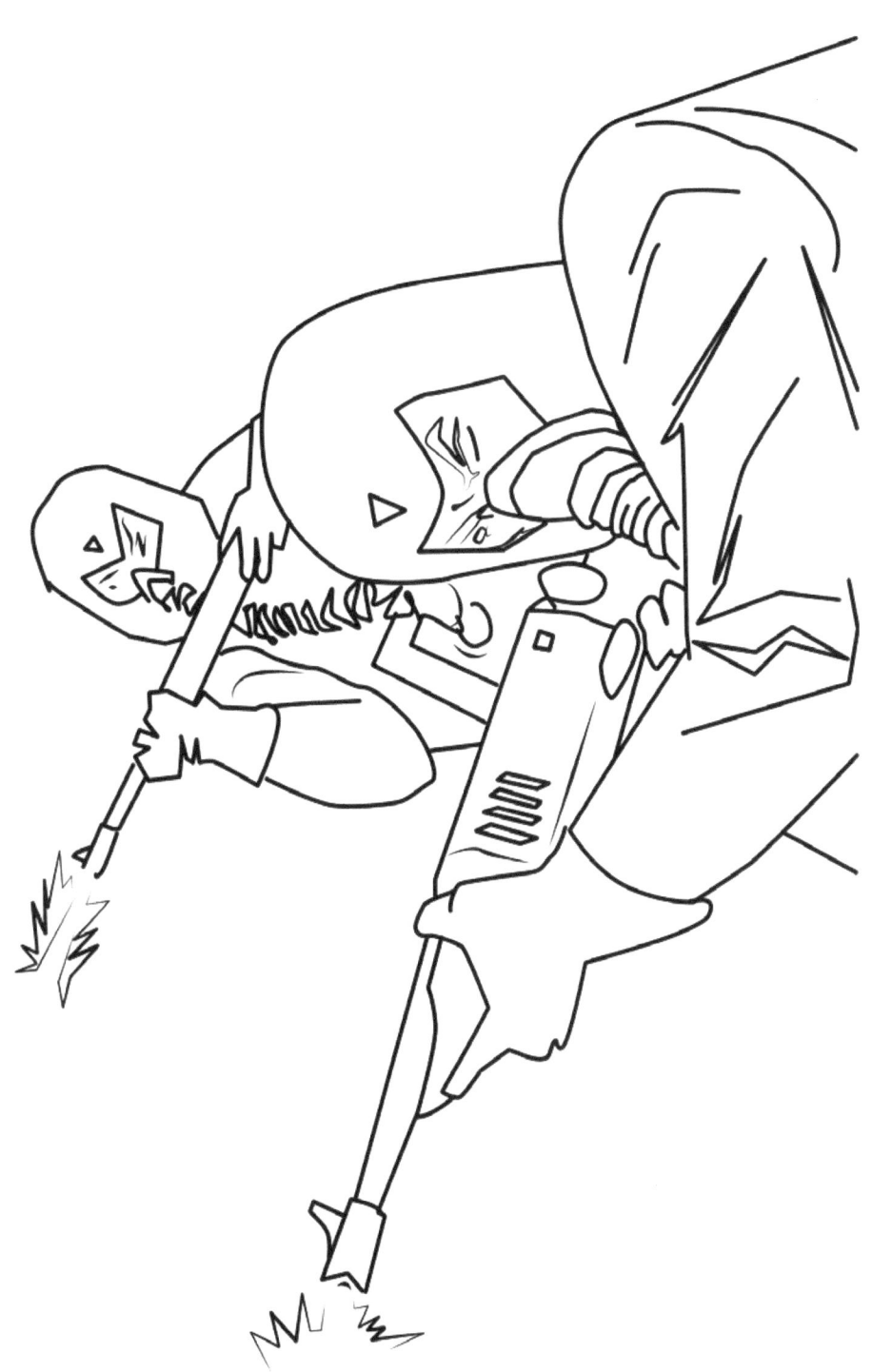

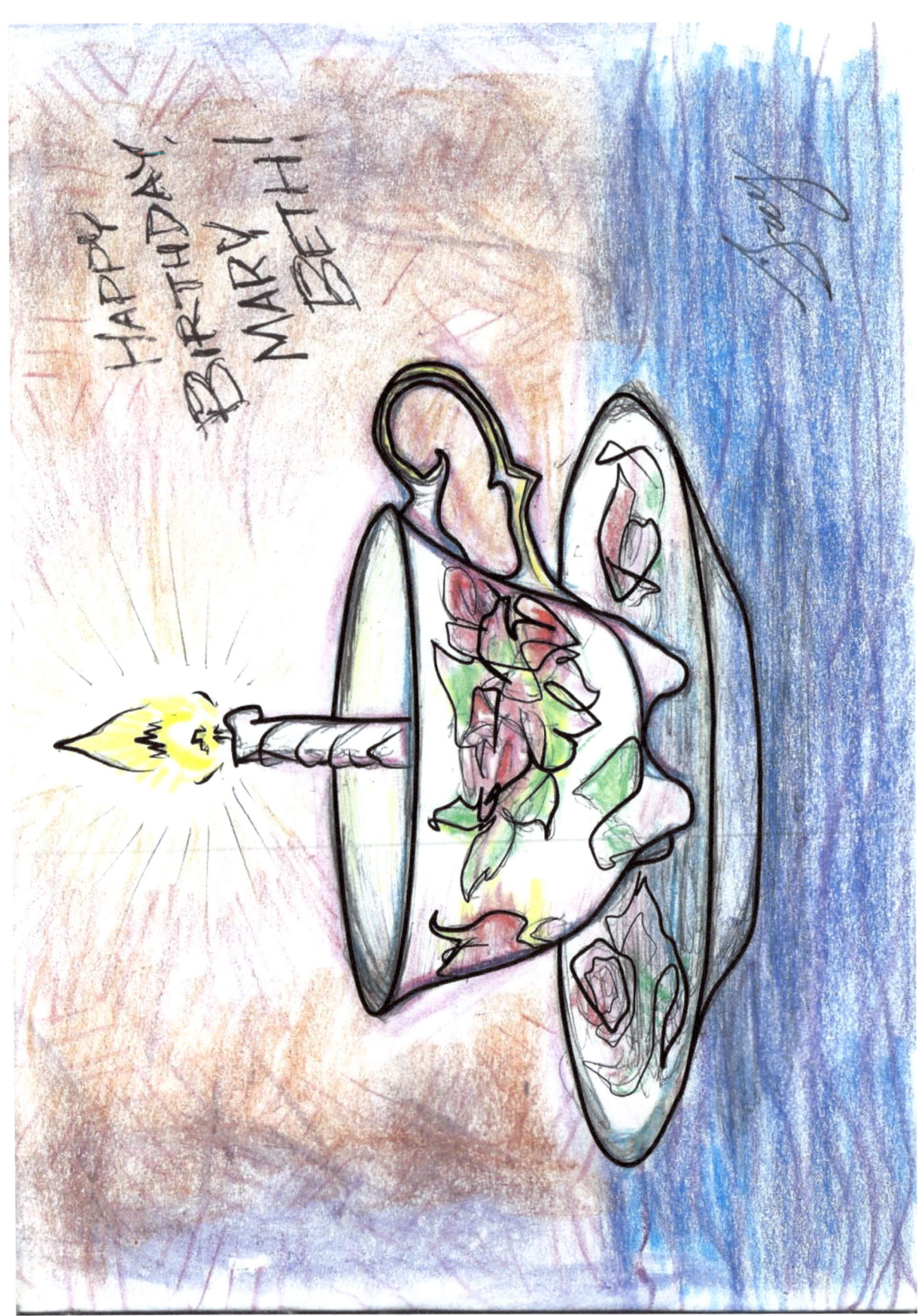

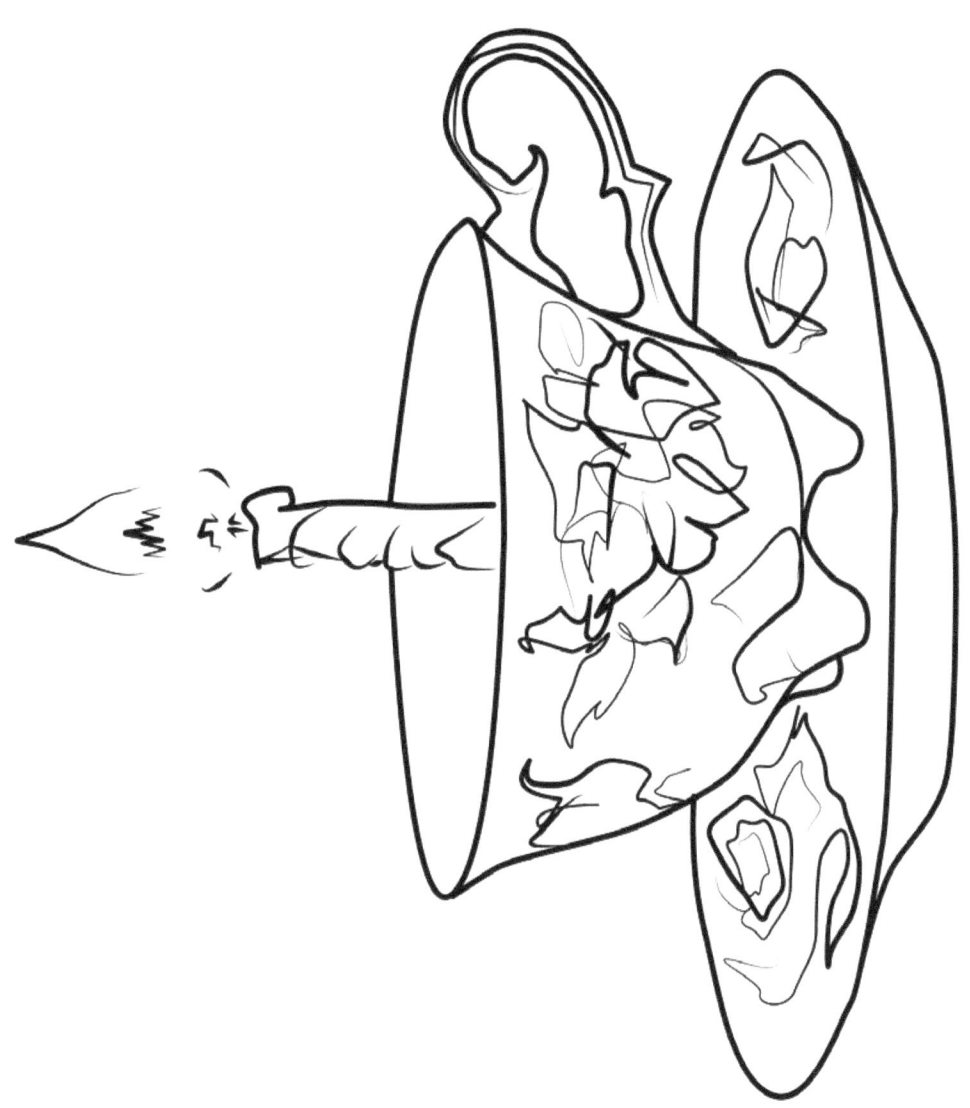

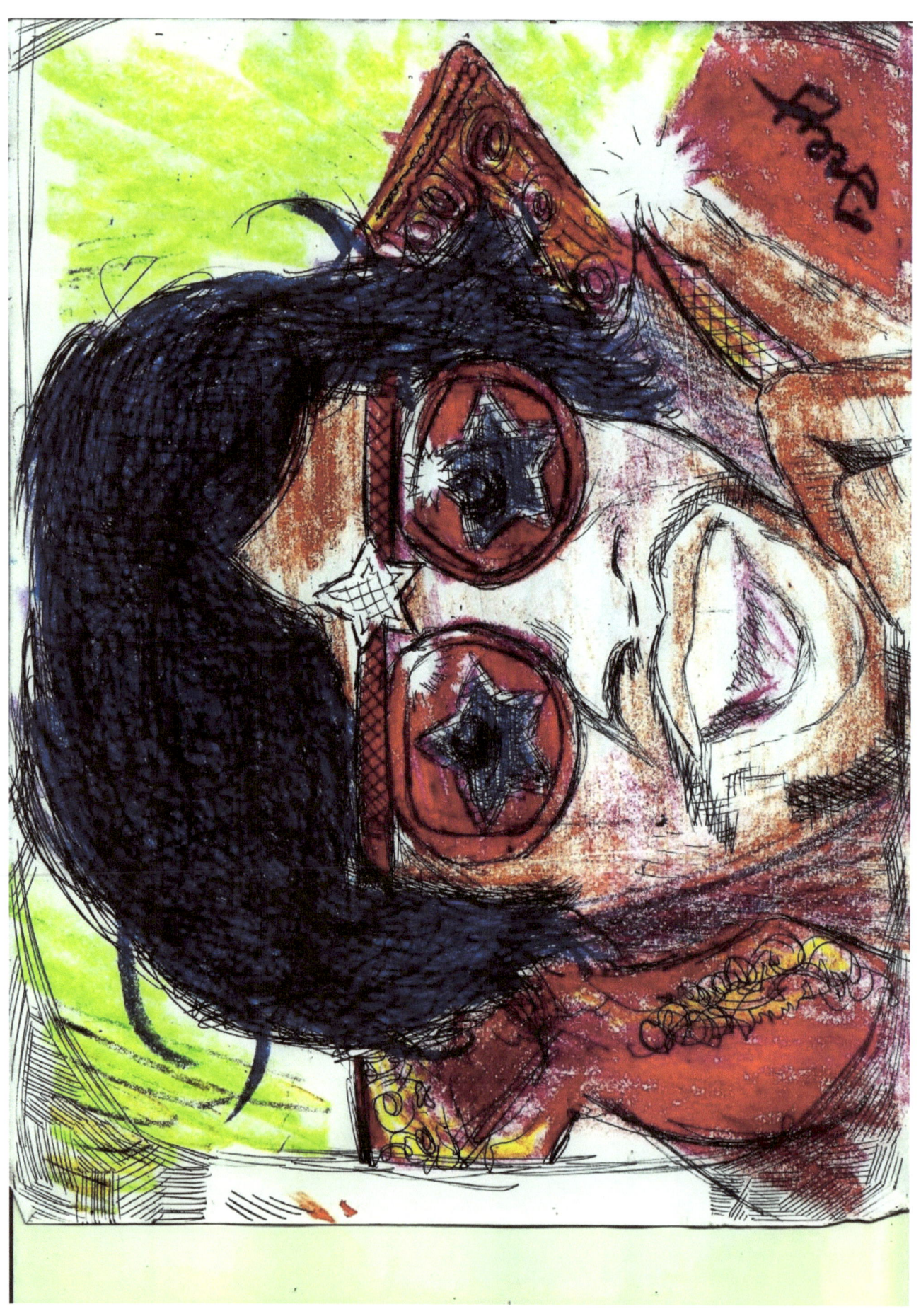

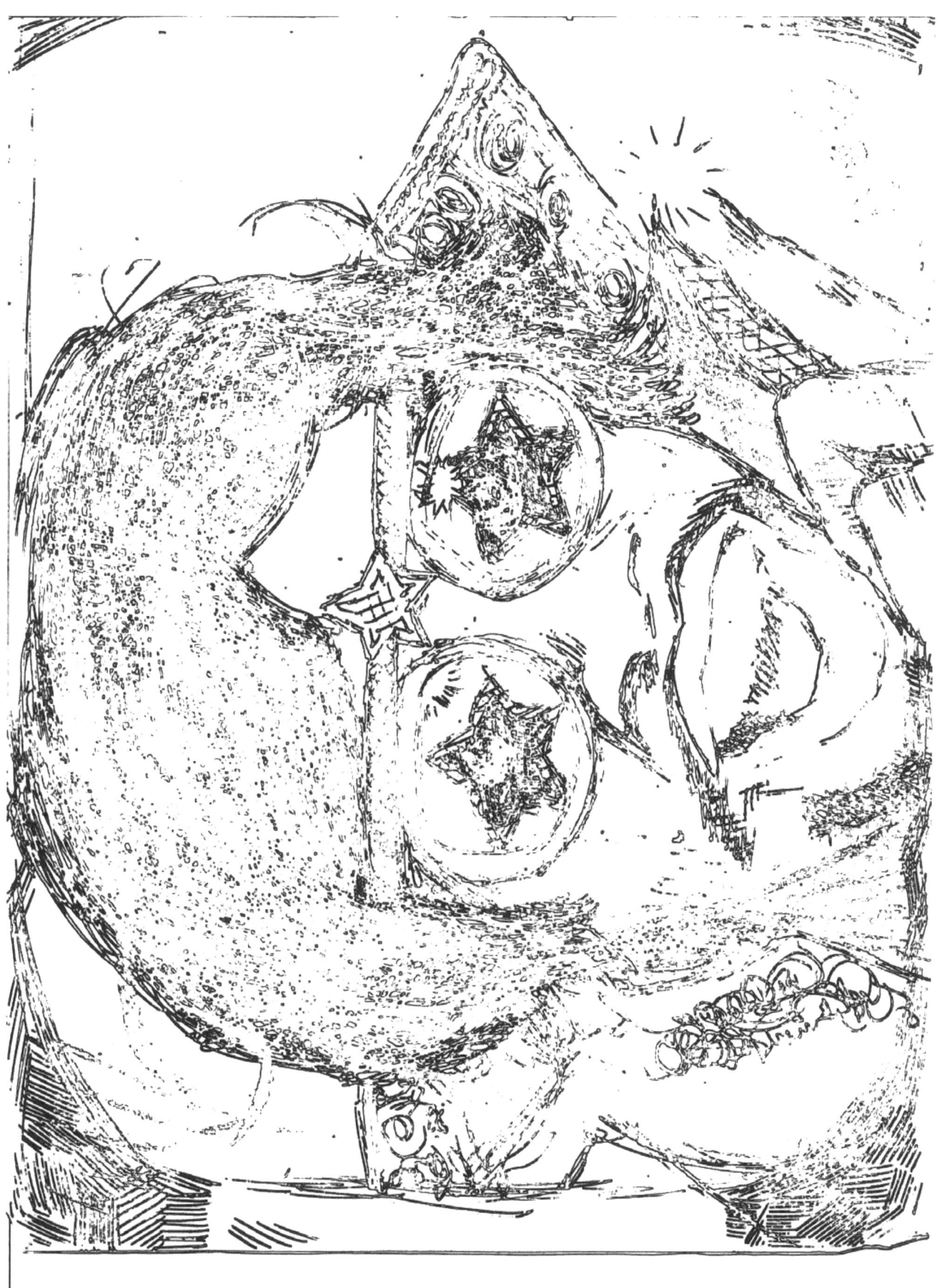

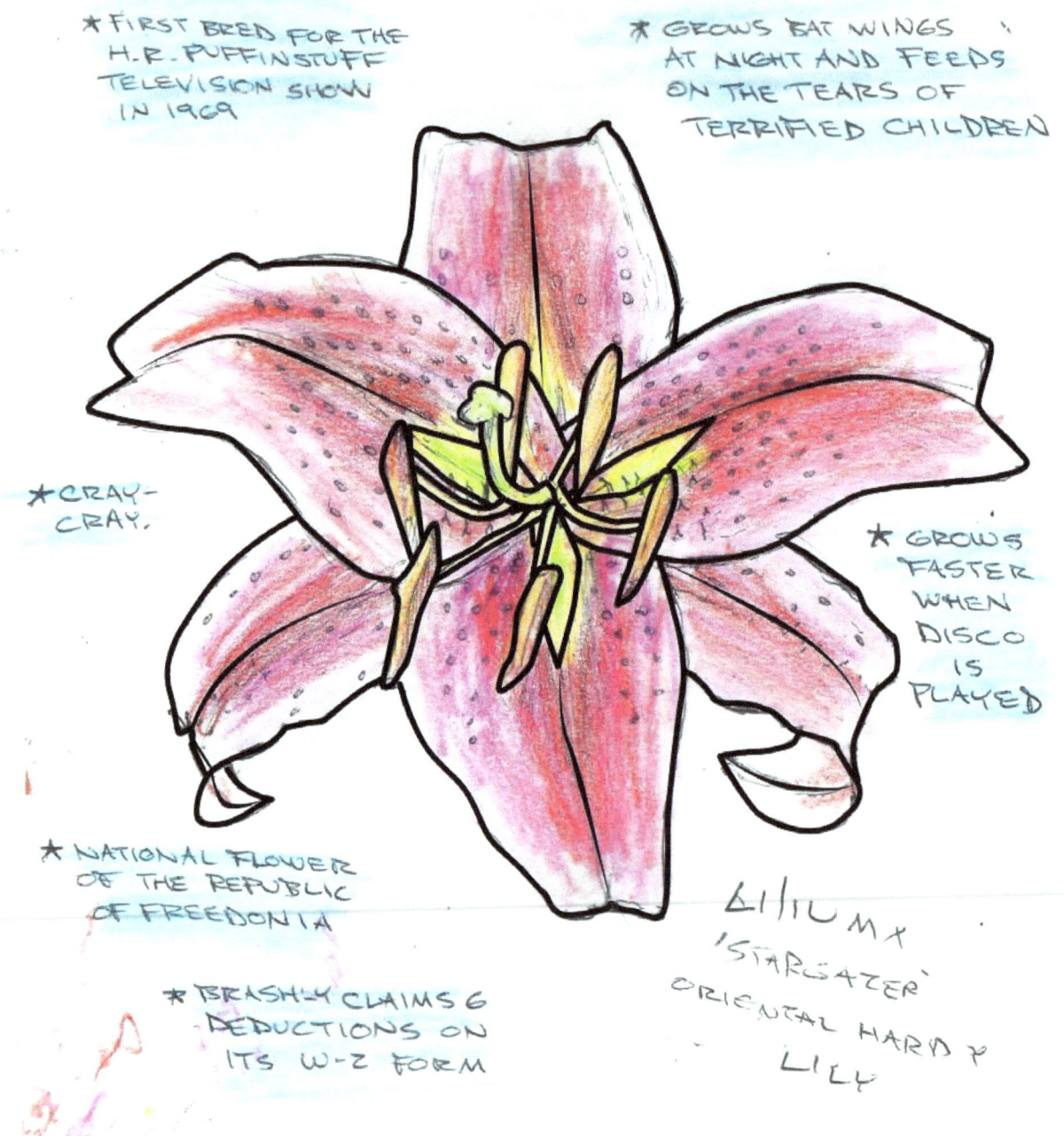

* FIRST BRED FOR THE H.R. PUFFINSTUFF TELEVISION SHOW IN 1969

* GROWS BAT WINGS AT NIGHT AND FEEDS ON THE TEARS OF TERRIFIED CHILDREN

* CRAY-CRAY.

* GROWS FASTER WHEN DISCO IS PLAYED

* NATIONAL FLOWER OF THE REPUBLIC OF FREEDONIA

* BRASHLY CLAIMS 6 DEDUCTIONS ON ITS W-2 FORM

LILIUM X 'STARGAZER' ORIENTAL HARDY LILY

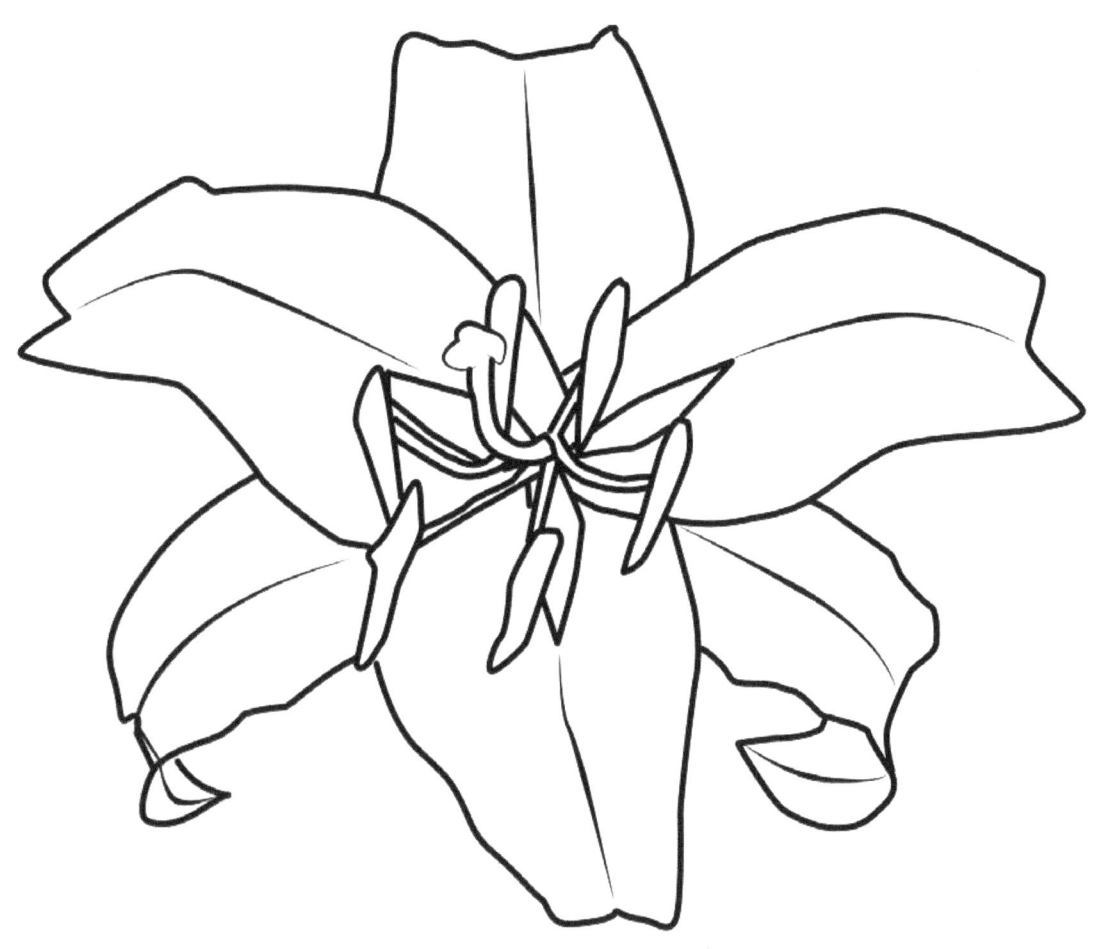

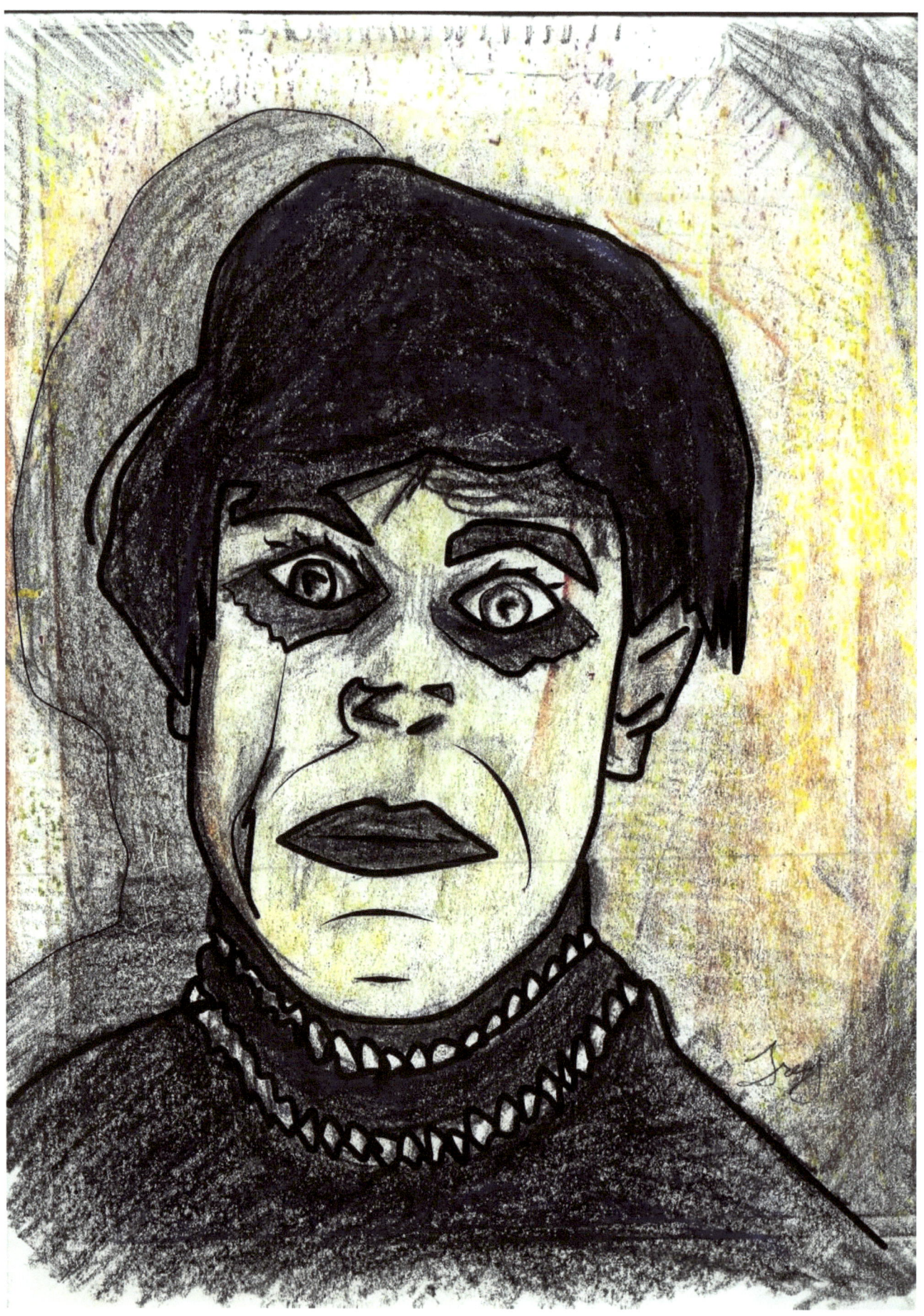

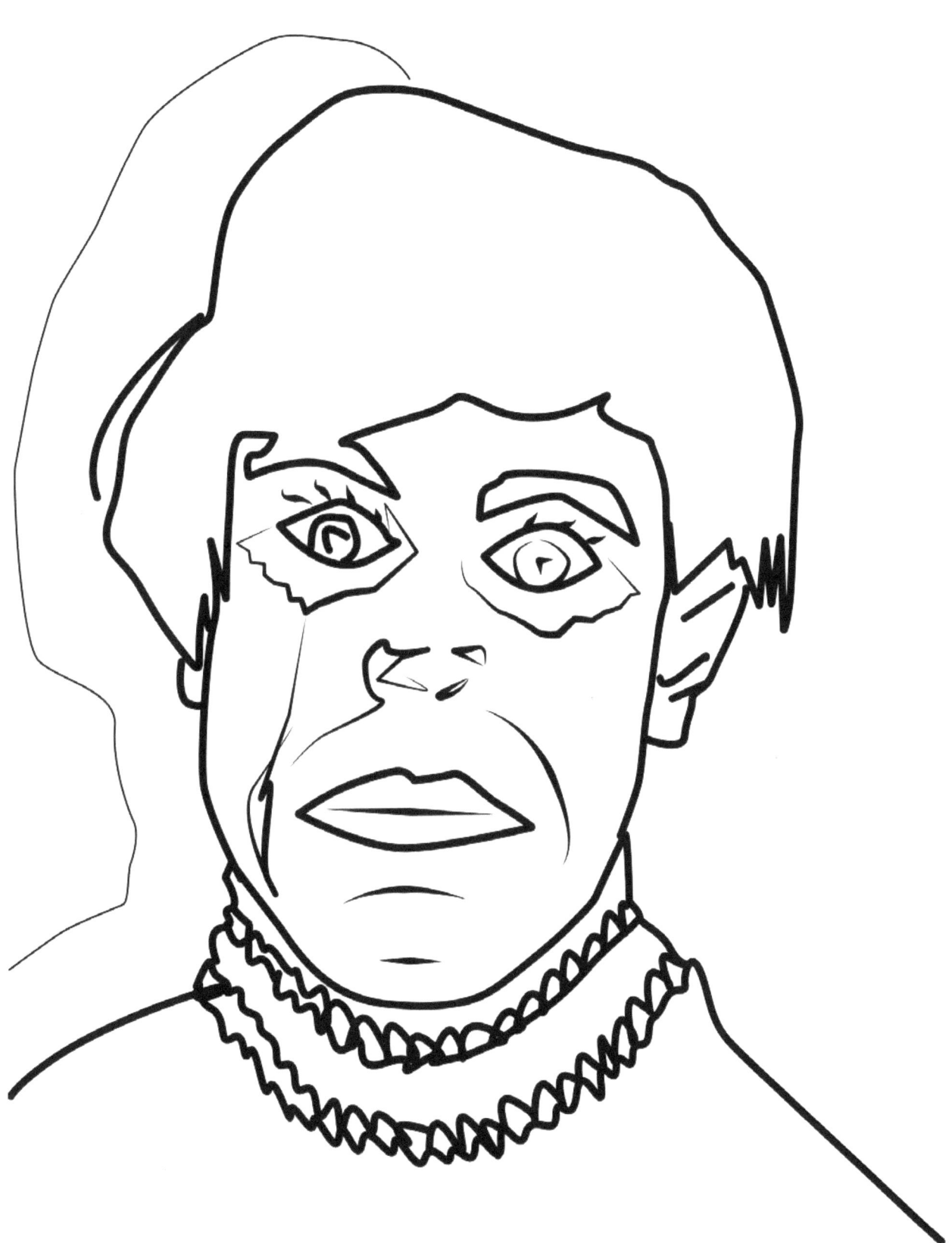

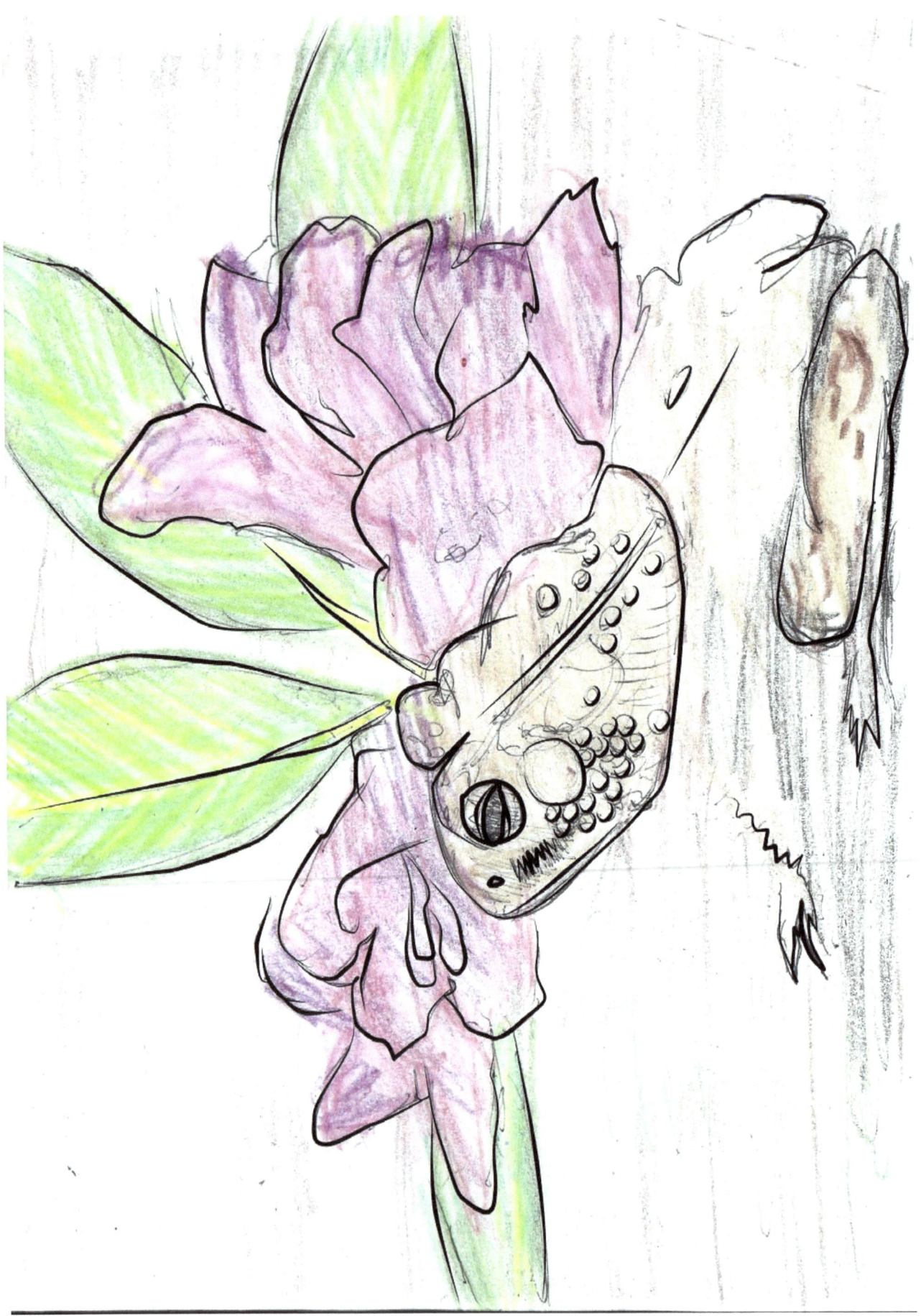

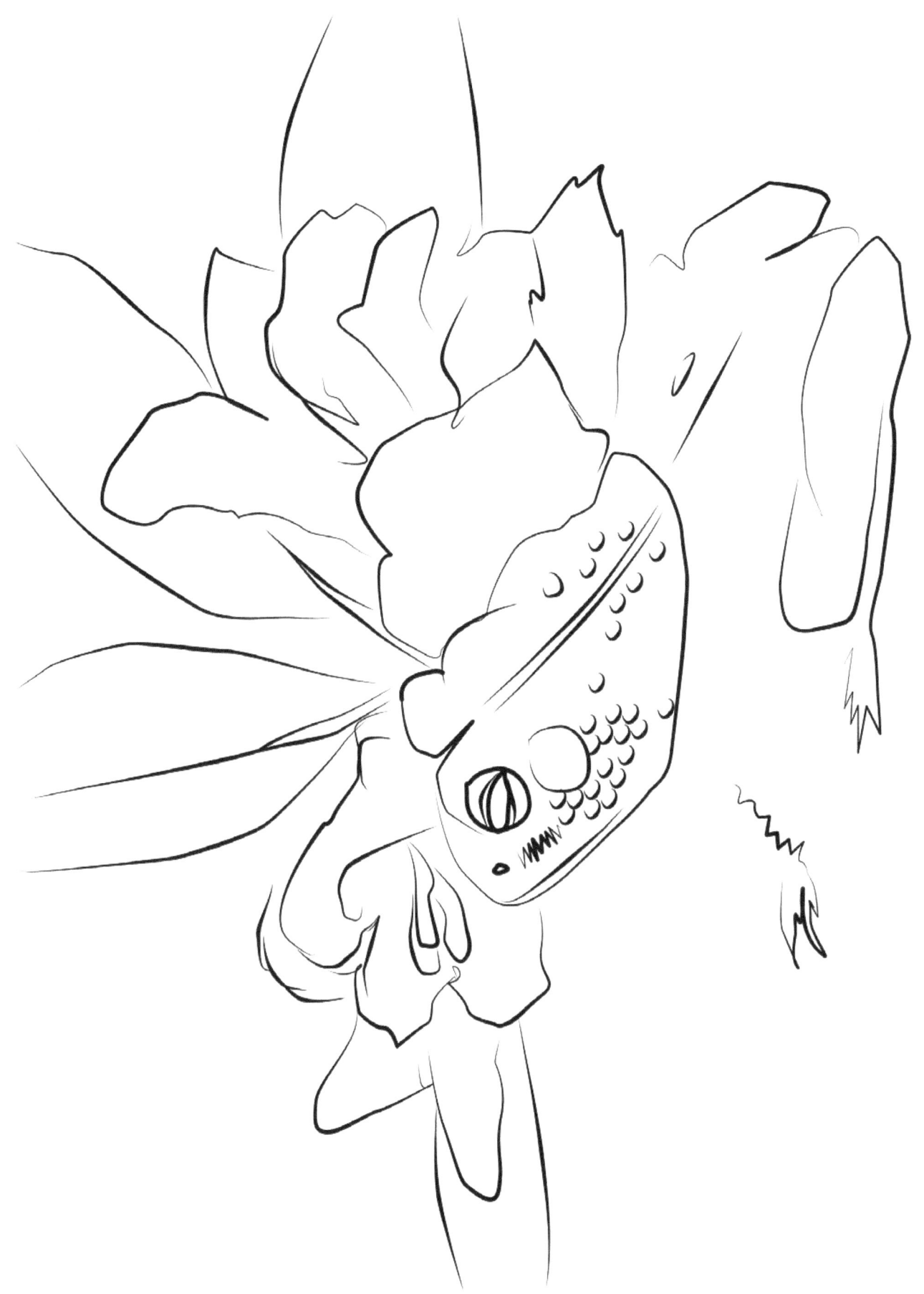

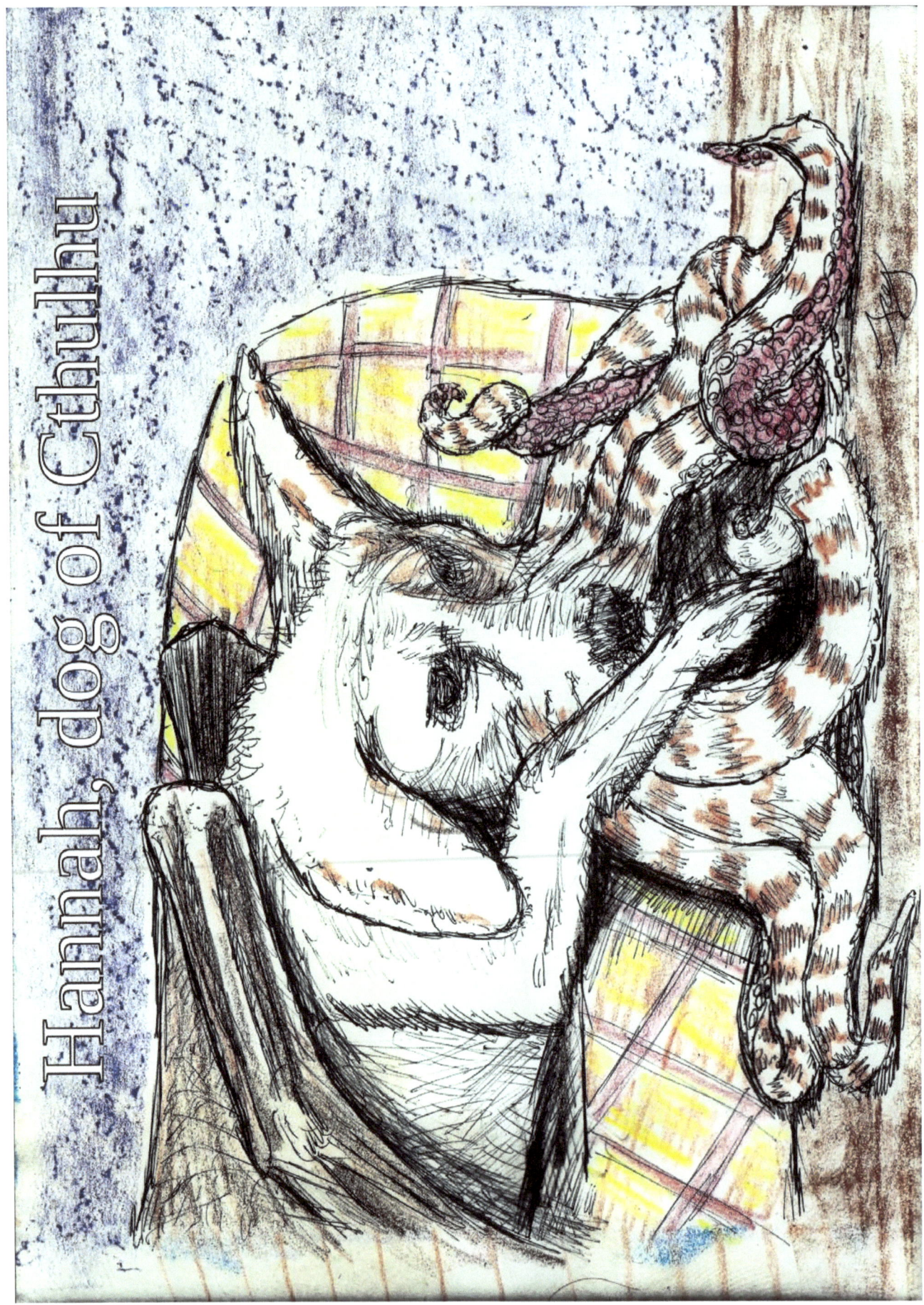
Hannah, dog of Cthulhu

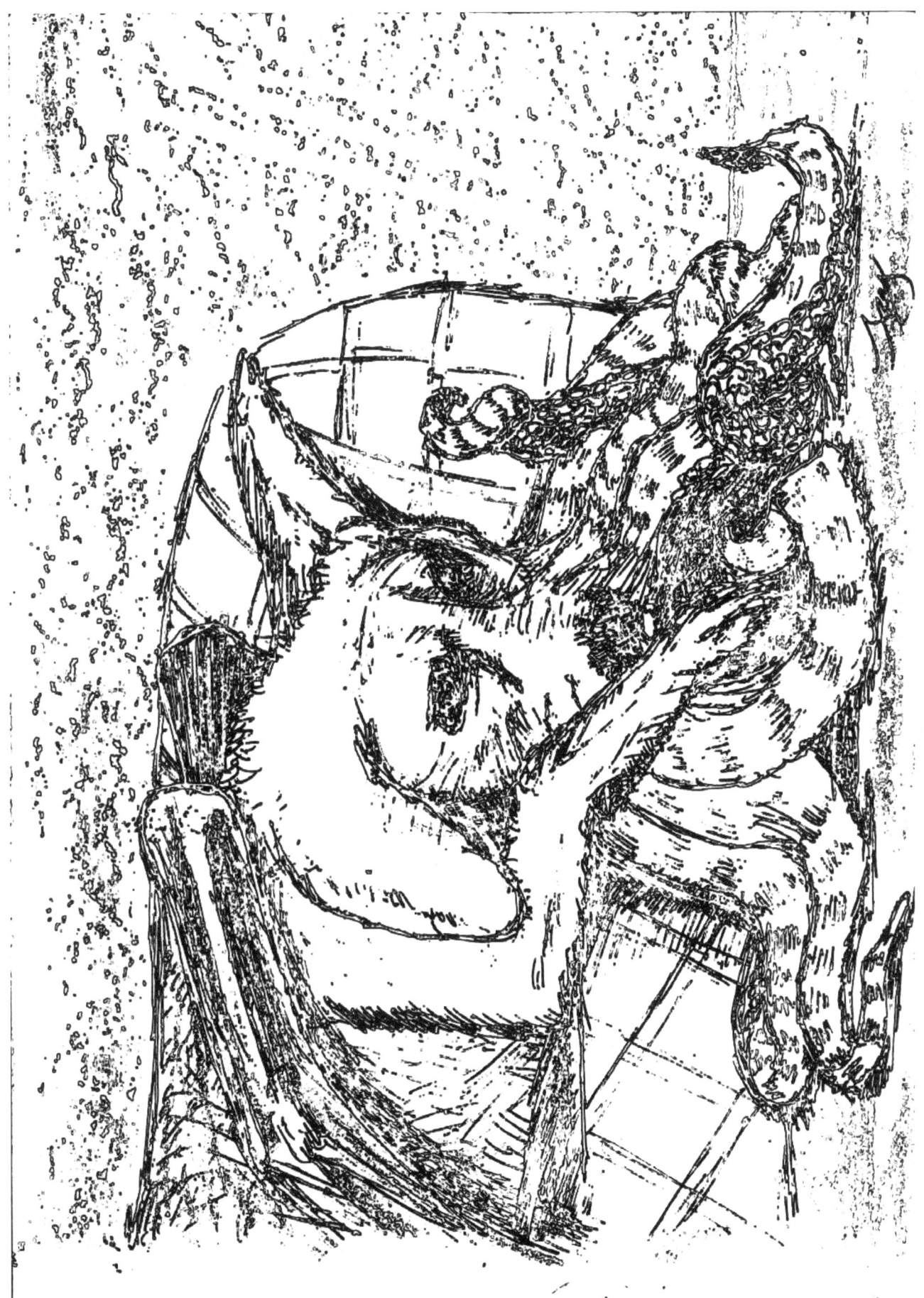

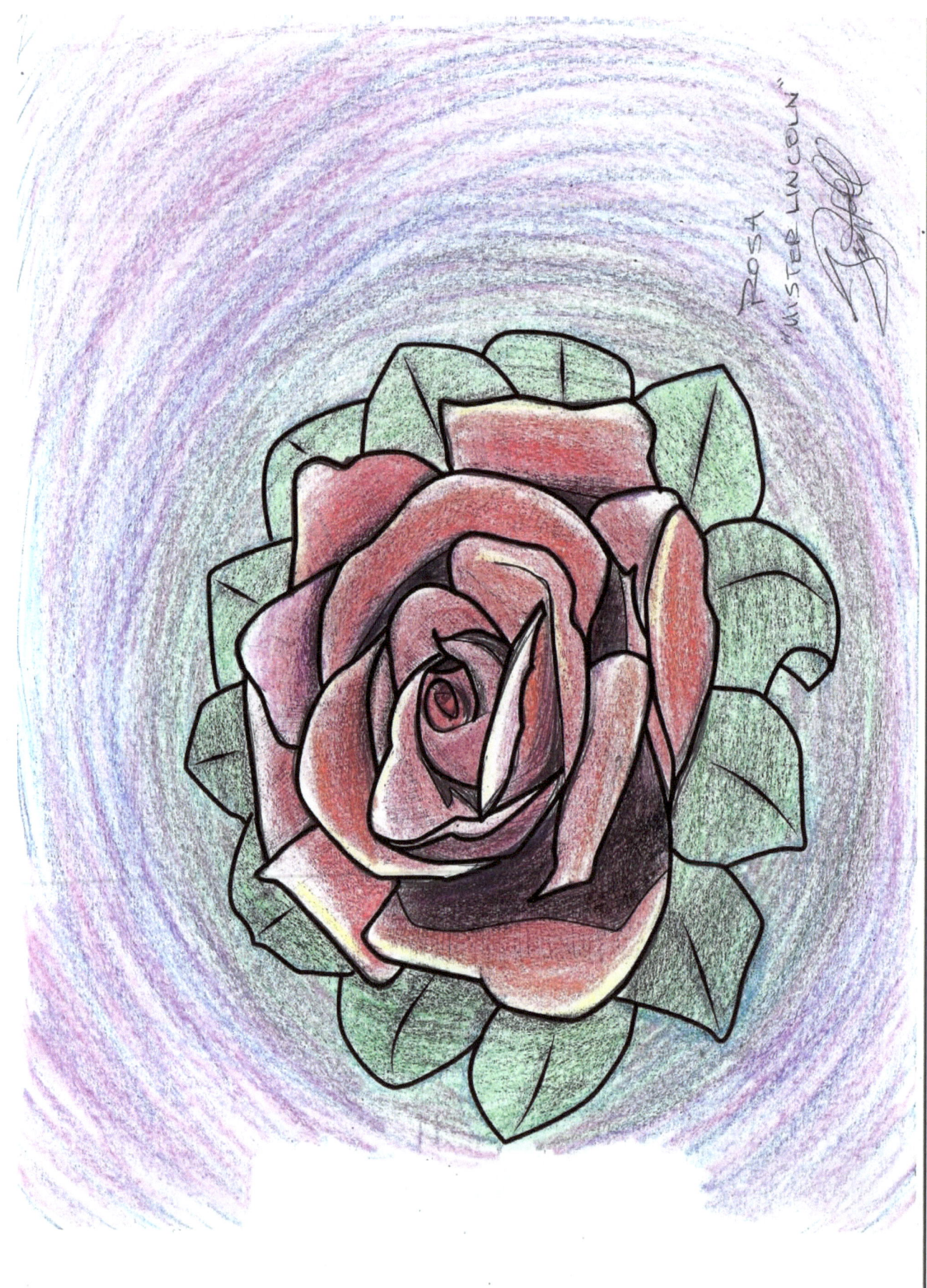

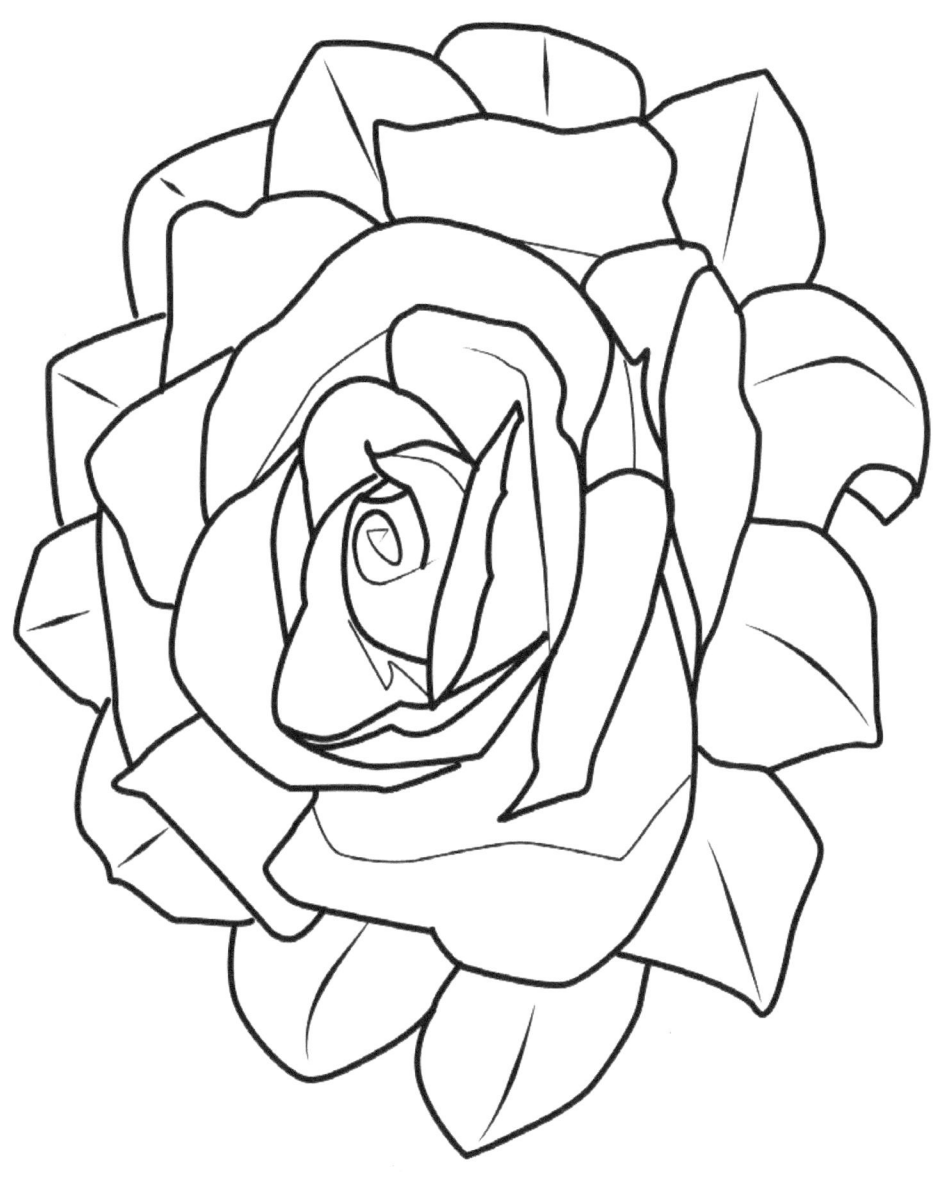

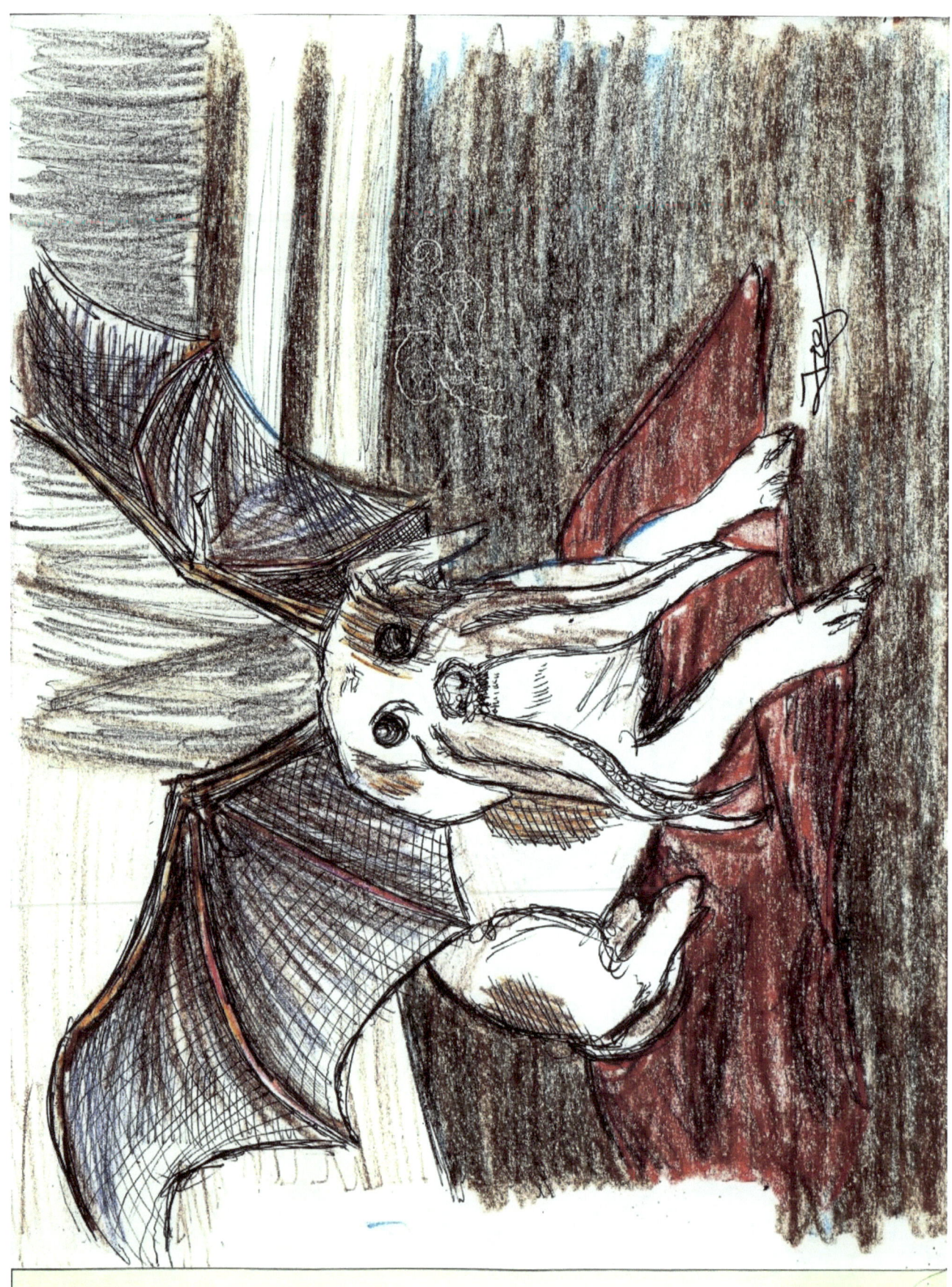

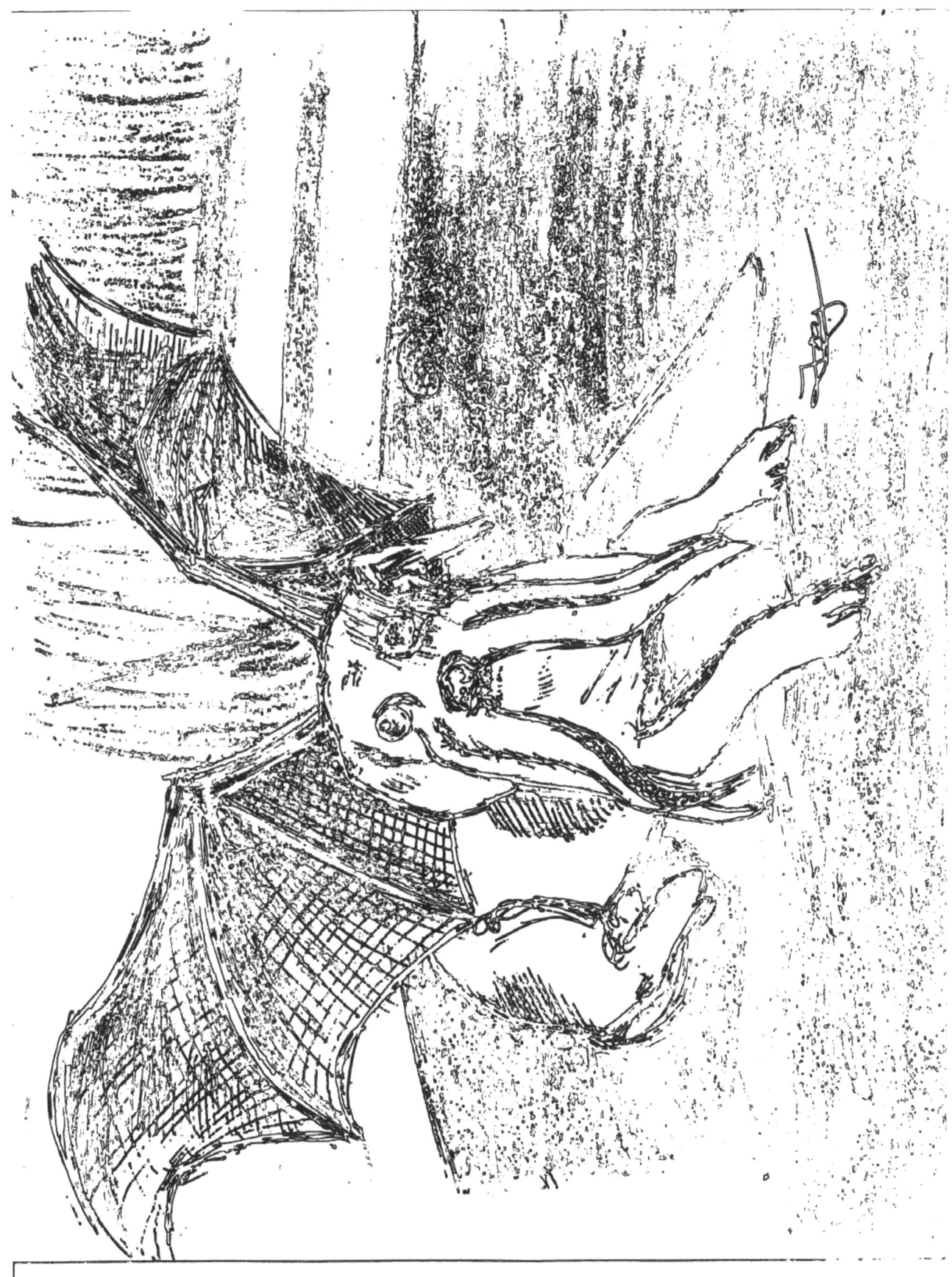

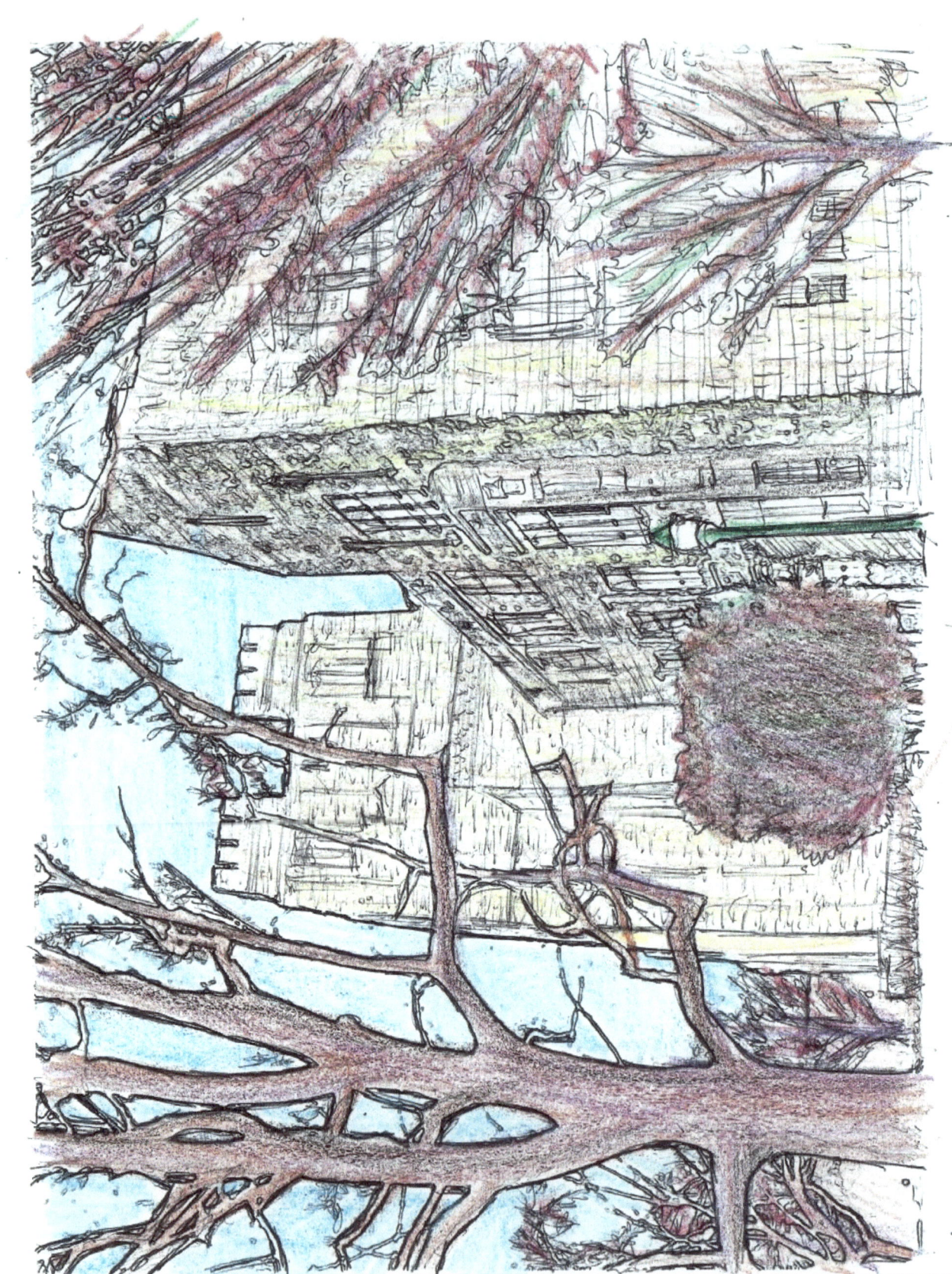

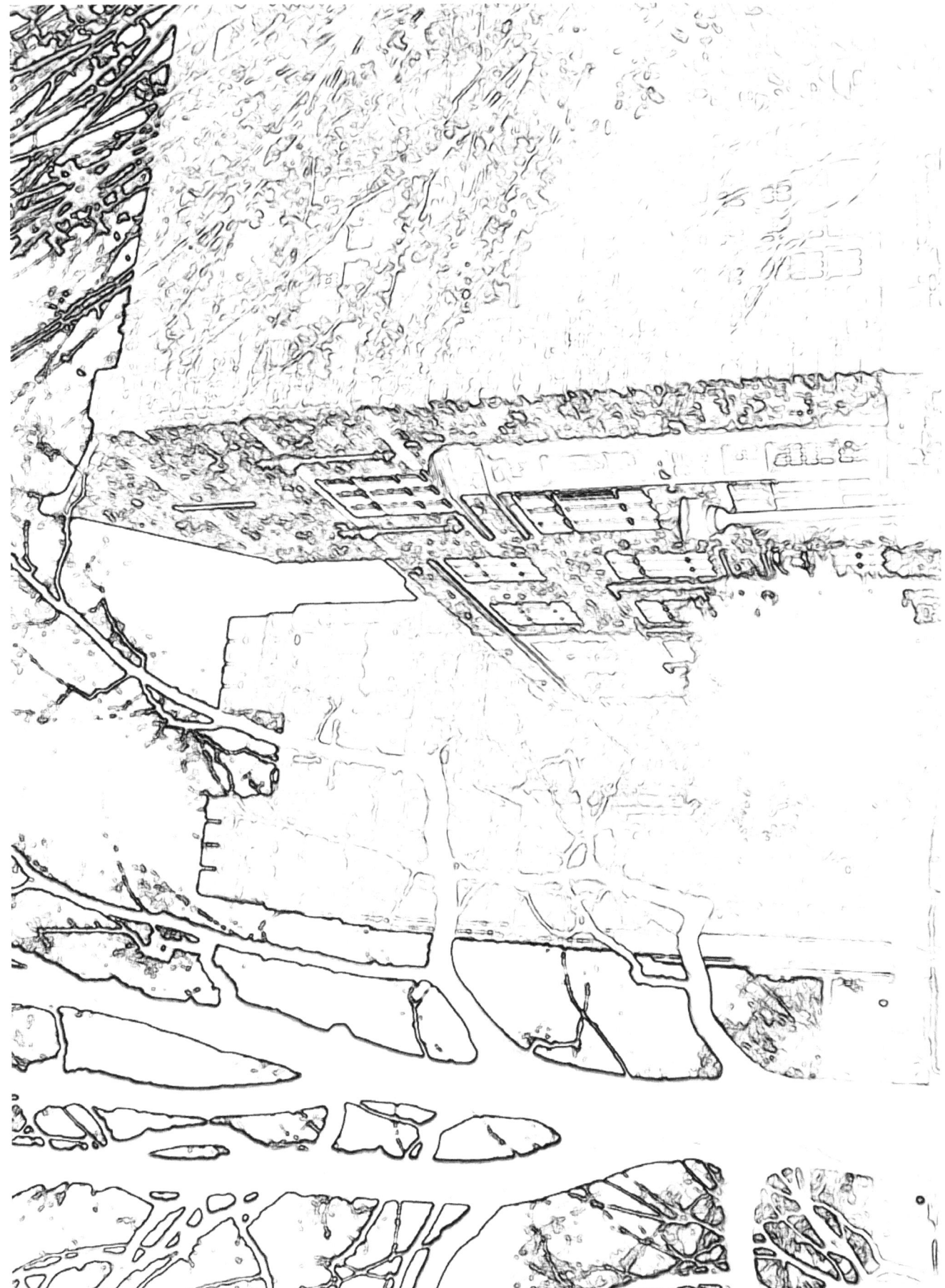

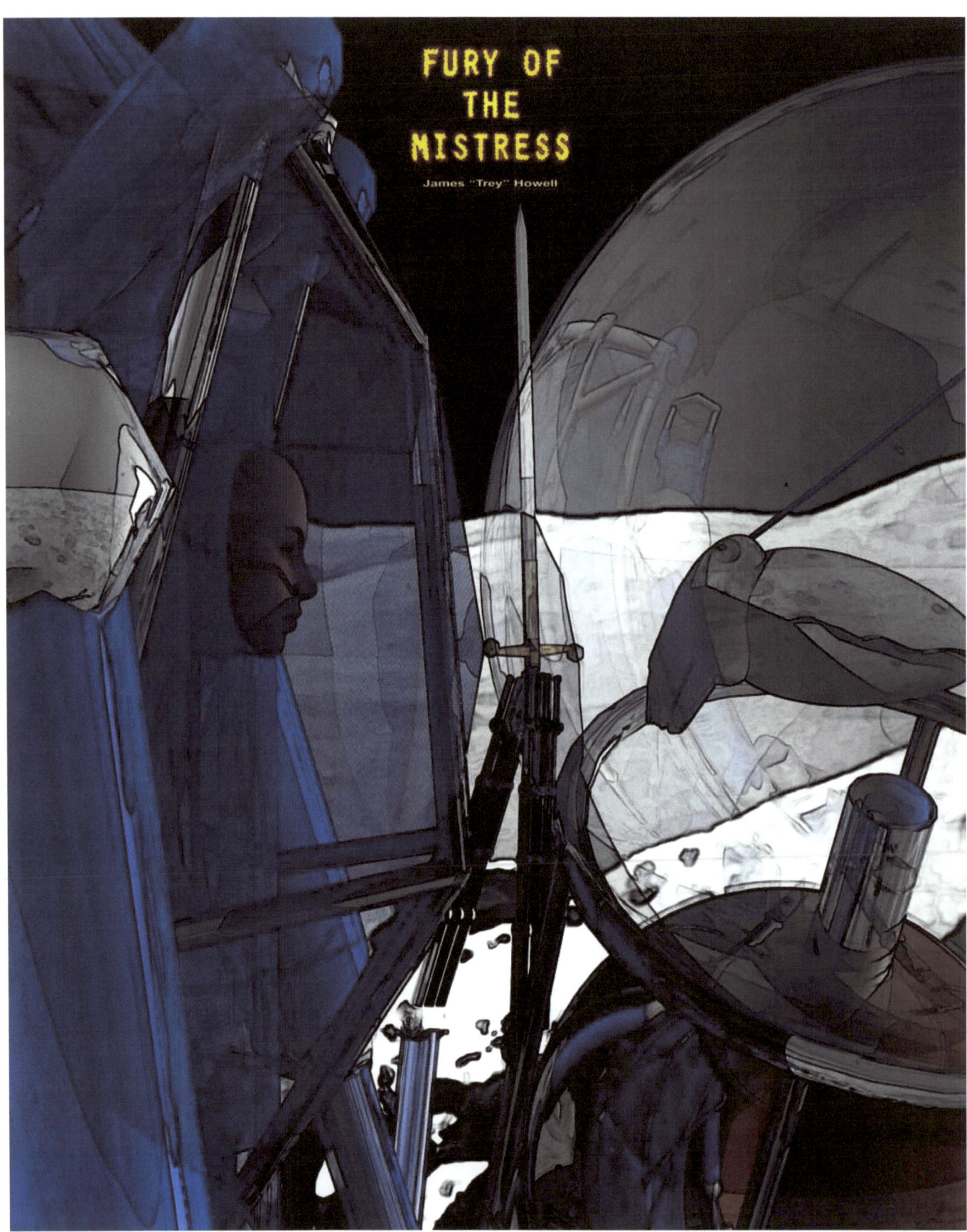

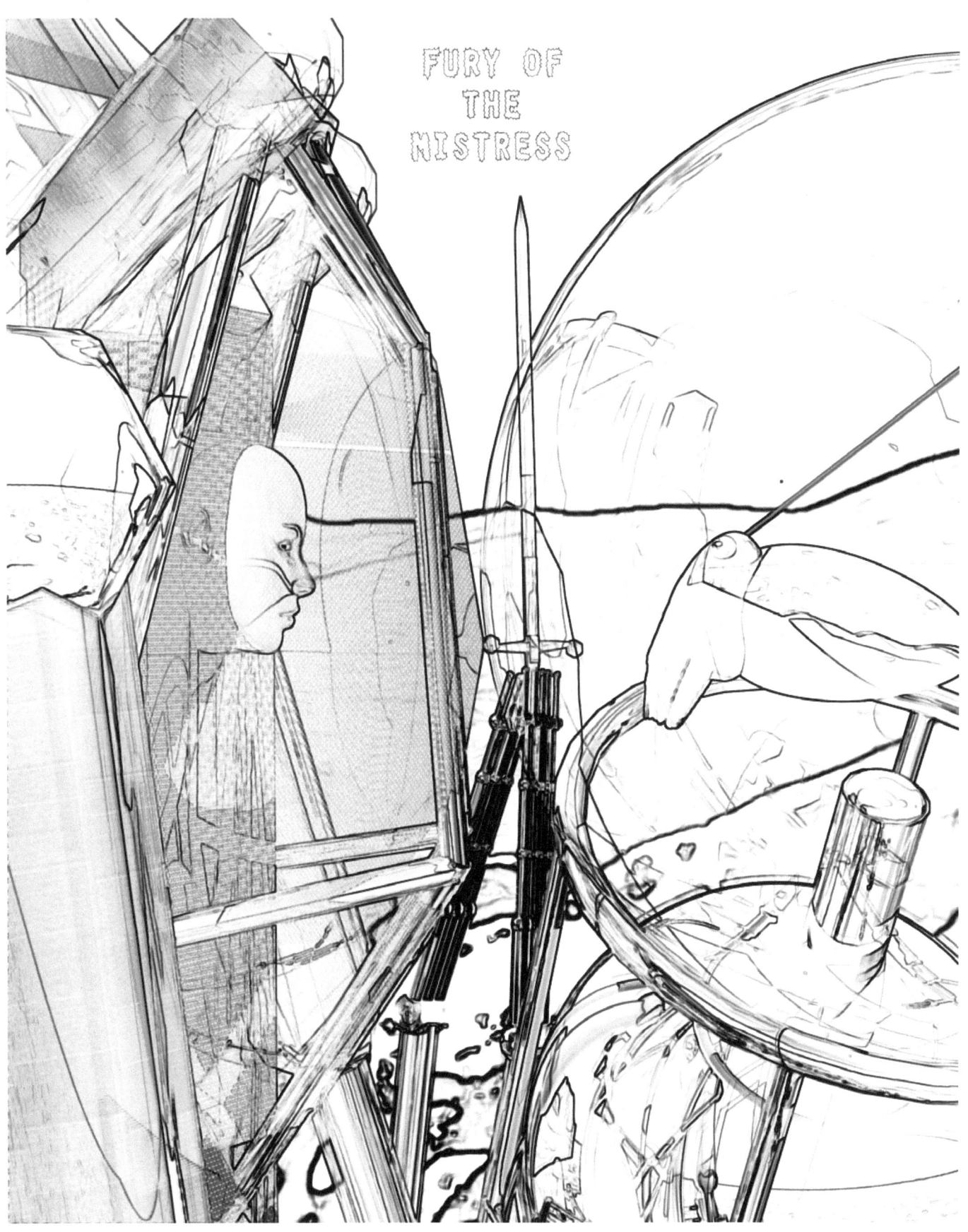

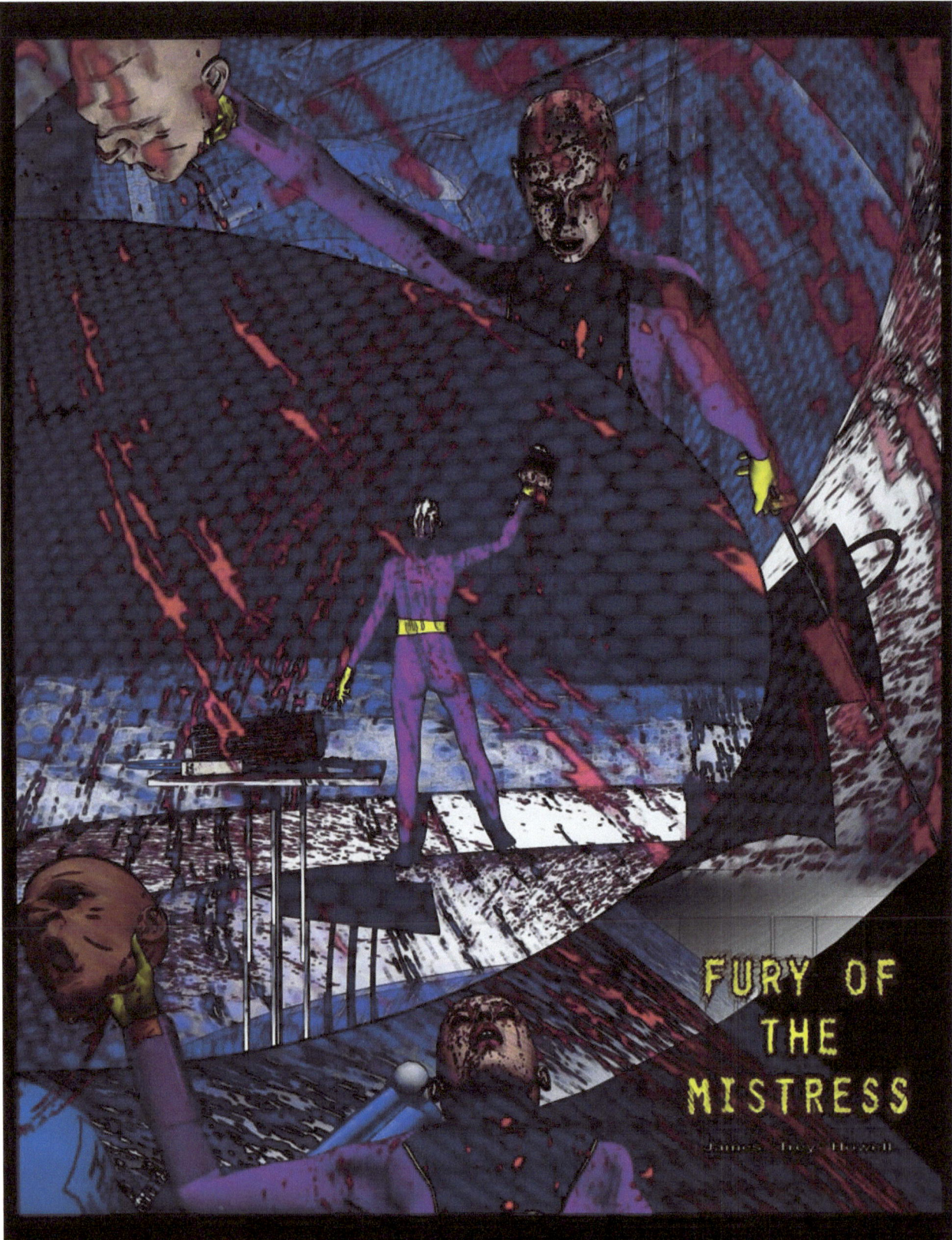

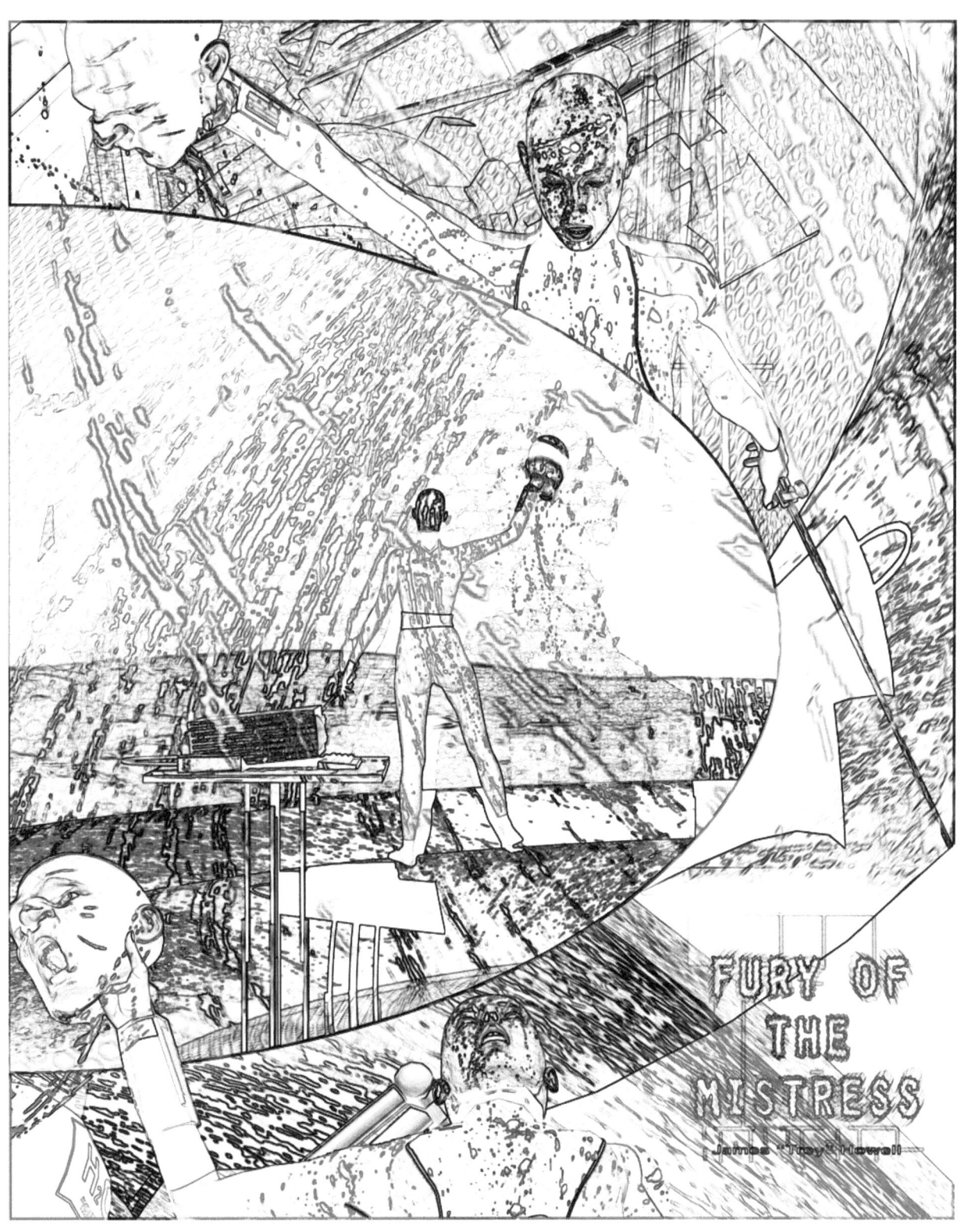

PART TWO: YOU'RE ON YOUR OWN

Wow, you must be awesome at coloring to make it here! Unless you cheated and paged through the book first. I think that's cheating, anyway. Truth be told I'm not really familiar with the coloring rule-book, but I'm sure it's in there.

Here's some pictures that you're welcome to color in any way that you wish. Do what you want! I know it will kick ass, because everything is better with color. Unless you're color blind, in which case, everything is better with varying shades of gray. Unless you're blind… okay, I'm not sure I can make this worthwhile if that's the case, but rock on if you're trying anyway.

And as usual, if you're unhappy with unstructured play-time, you can go fly a kite. There's one right over there on the next page, so don't say I didn't make this book easy for you.

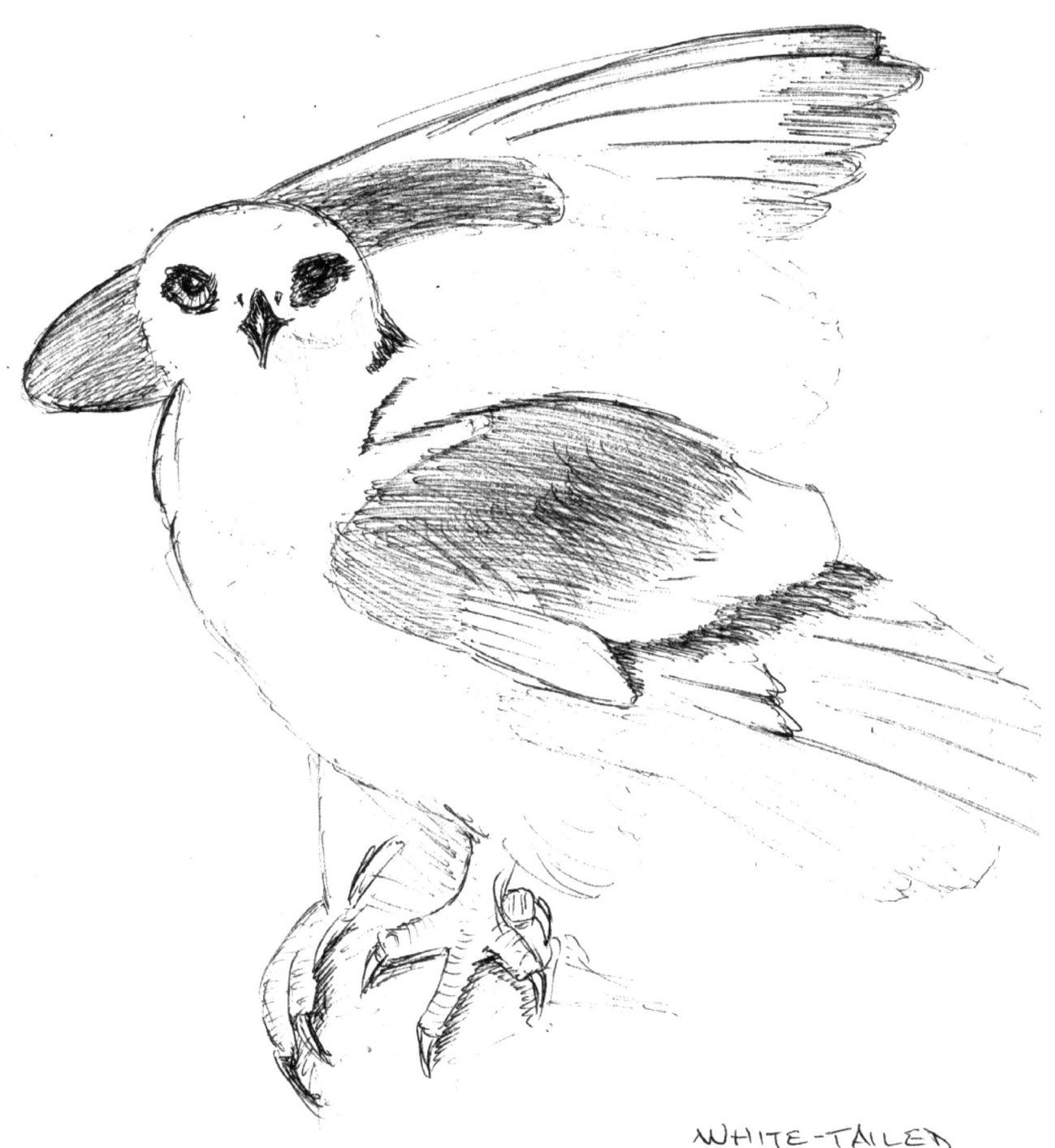

WHITE-TAILED KITE

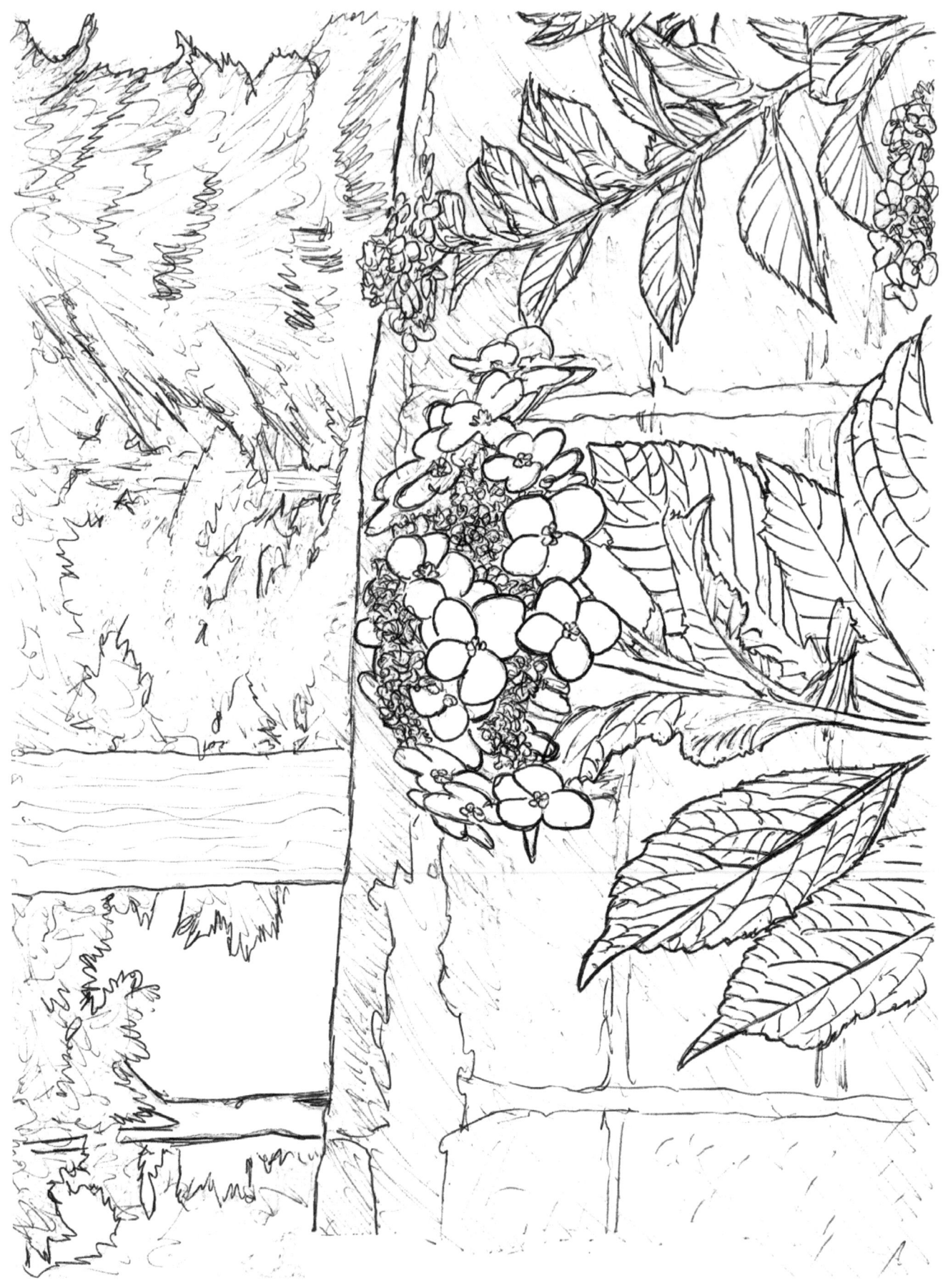

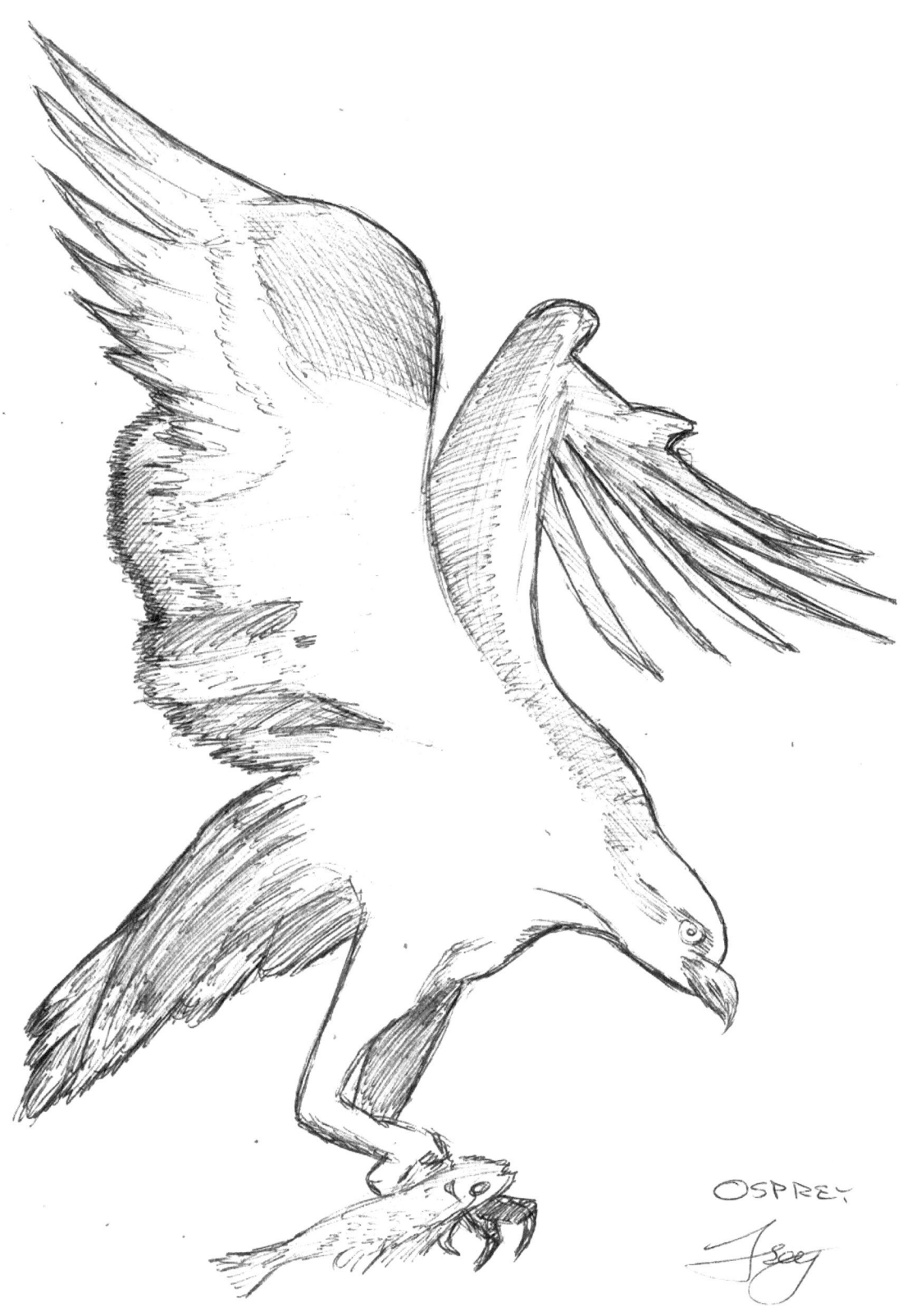

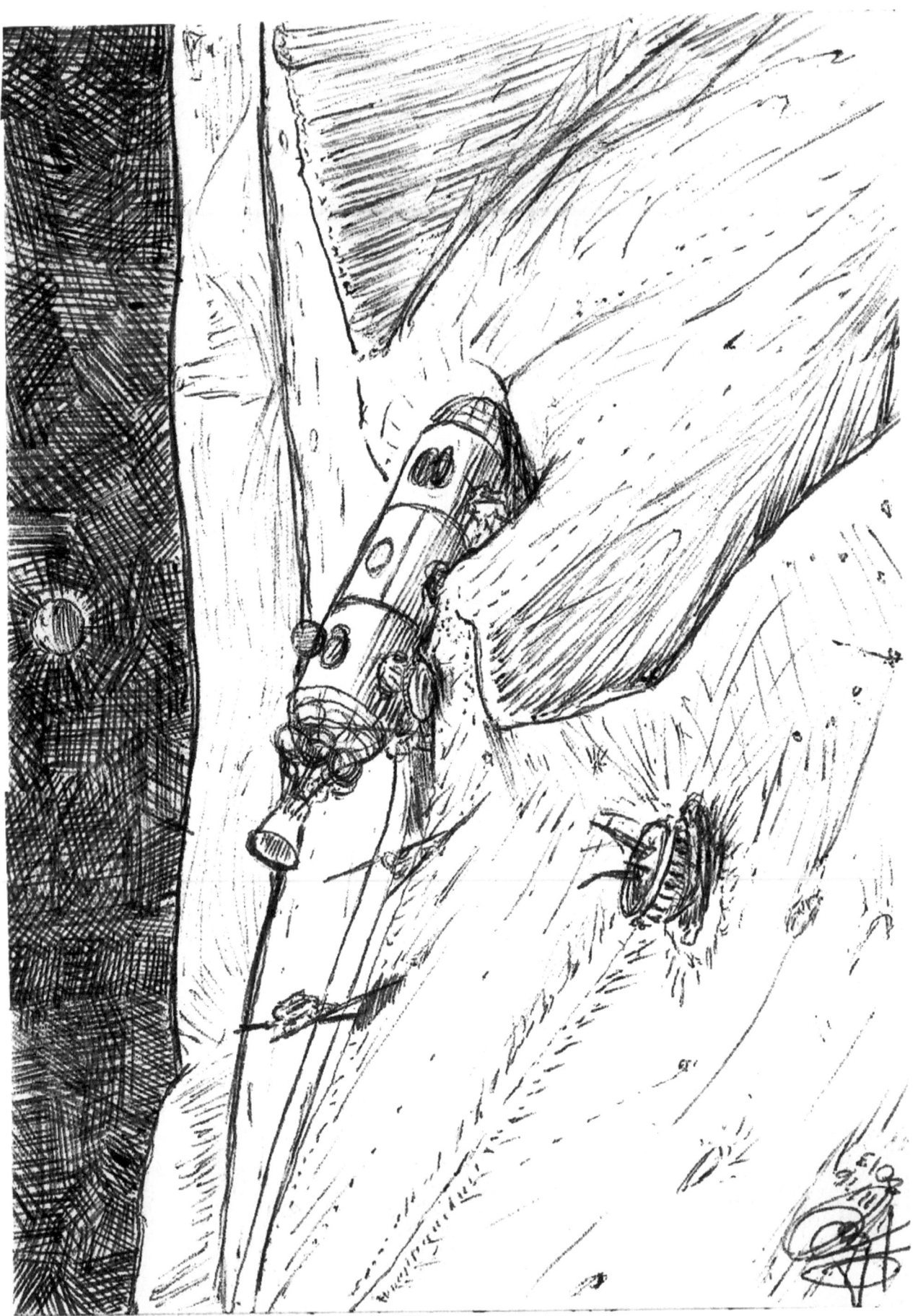

PART THREE: DO-OVERS

Who doesn't appreciate a second chance? Oh, you're that guy? Read the damned introduction—I've got something in there for you.

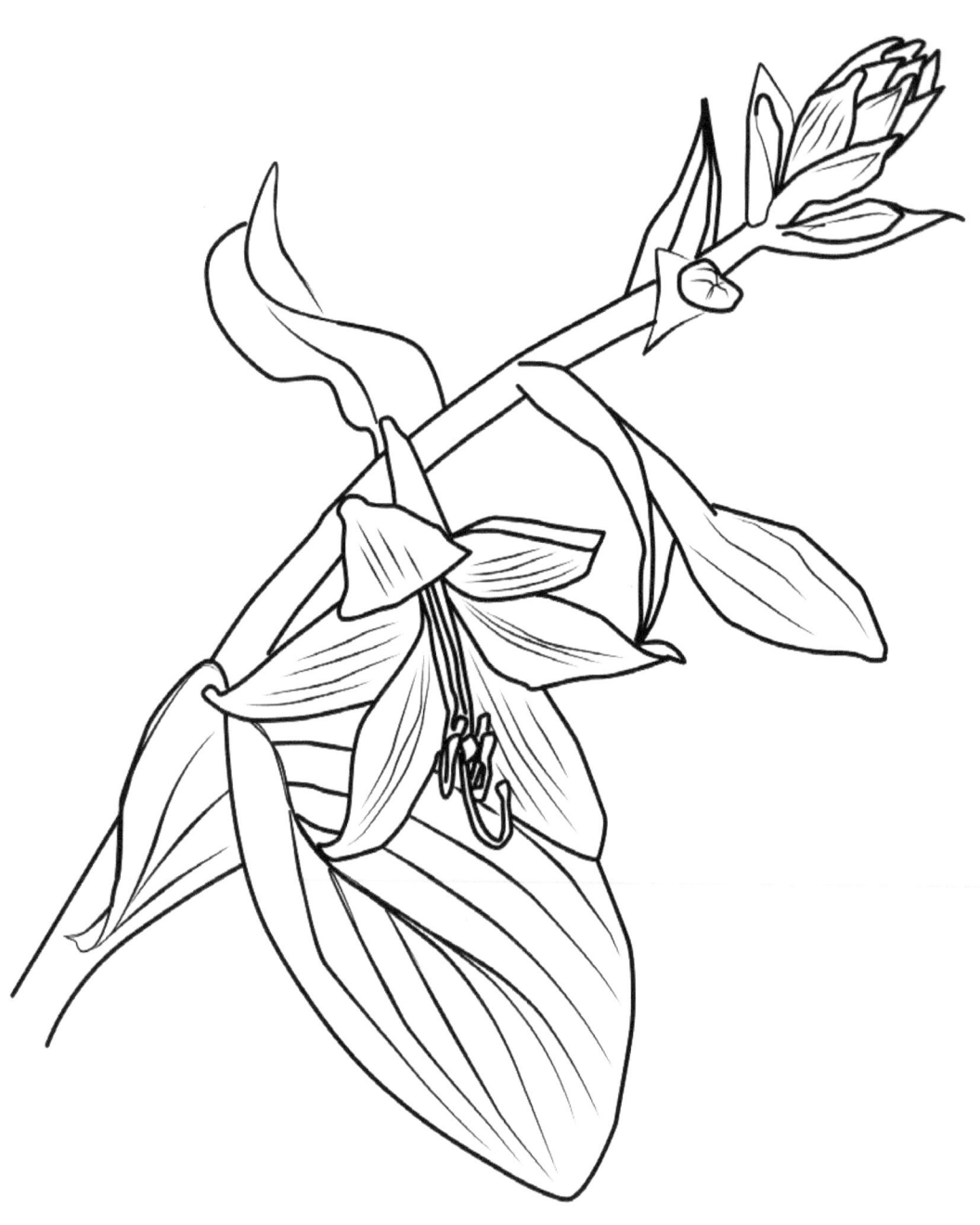

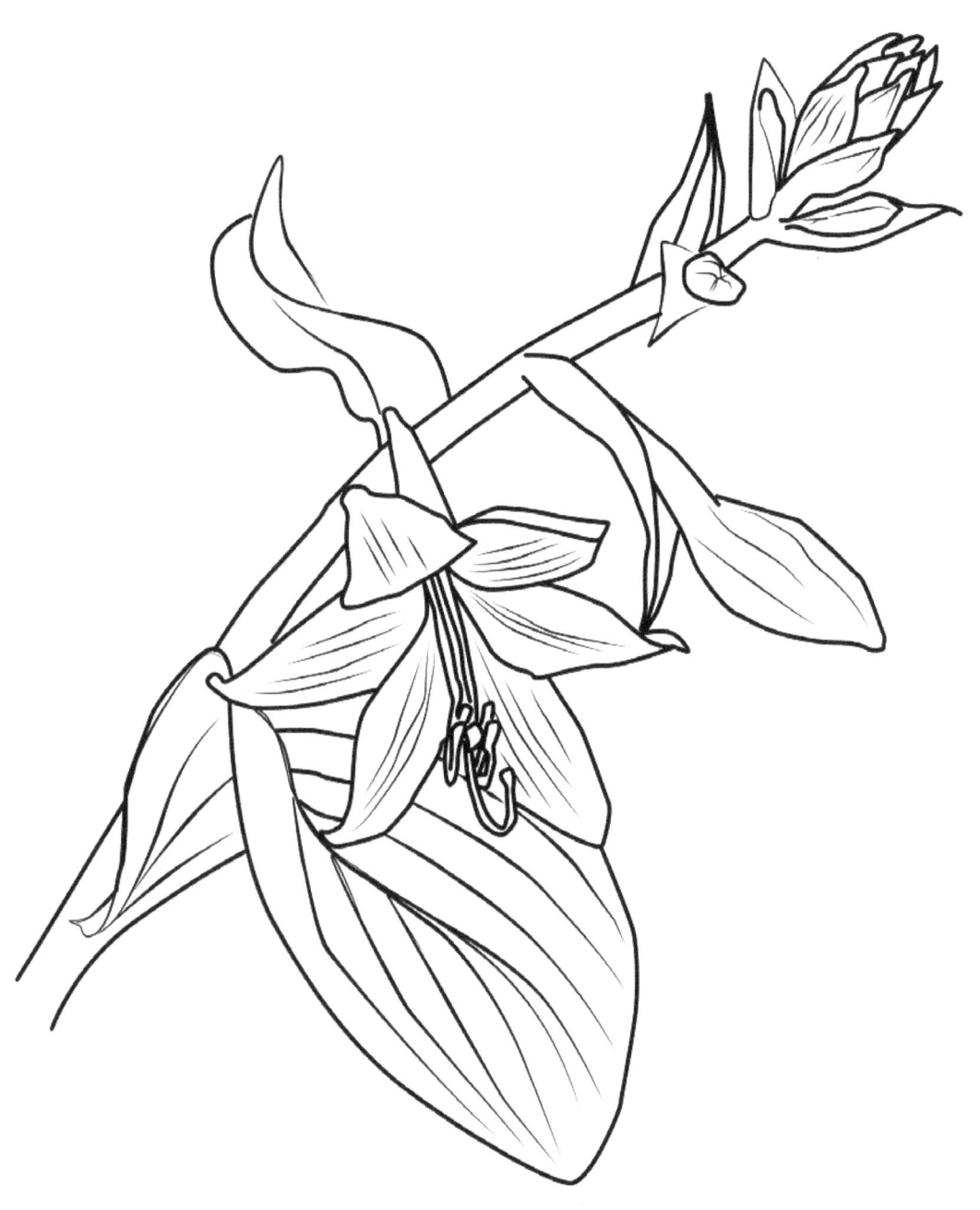

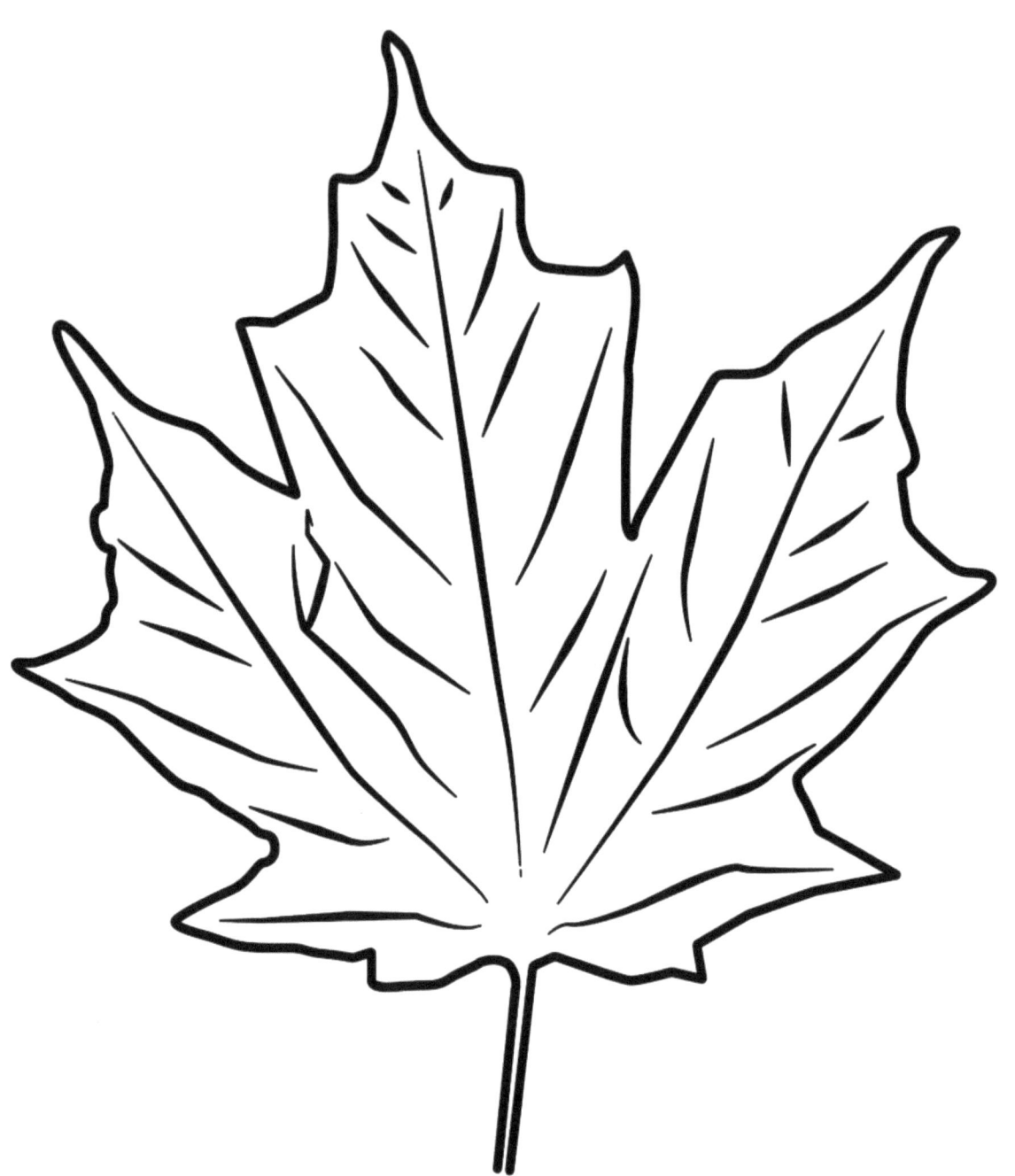

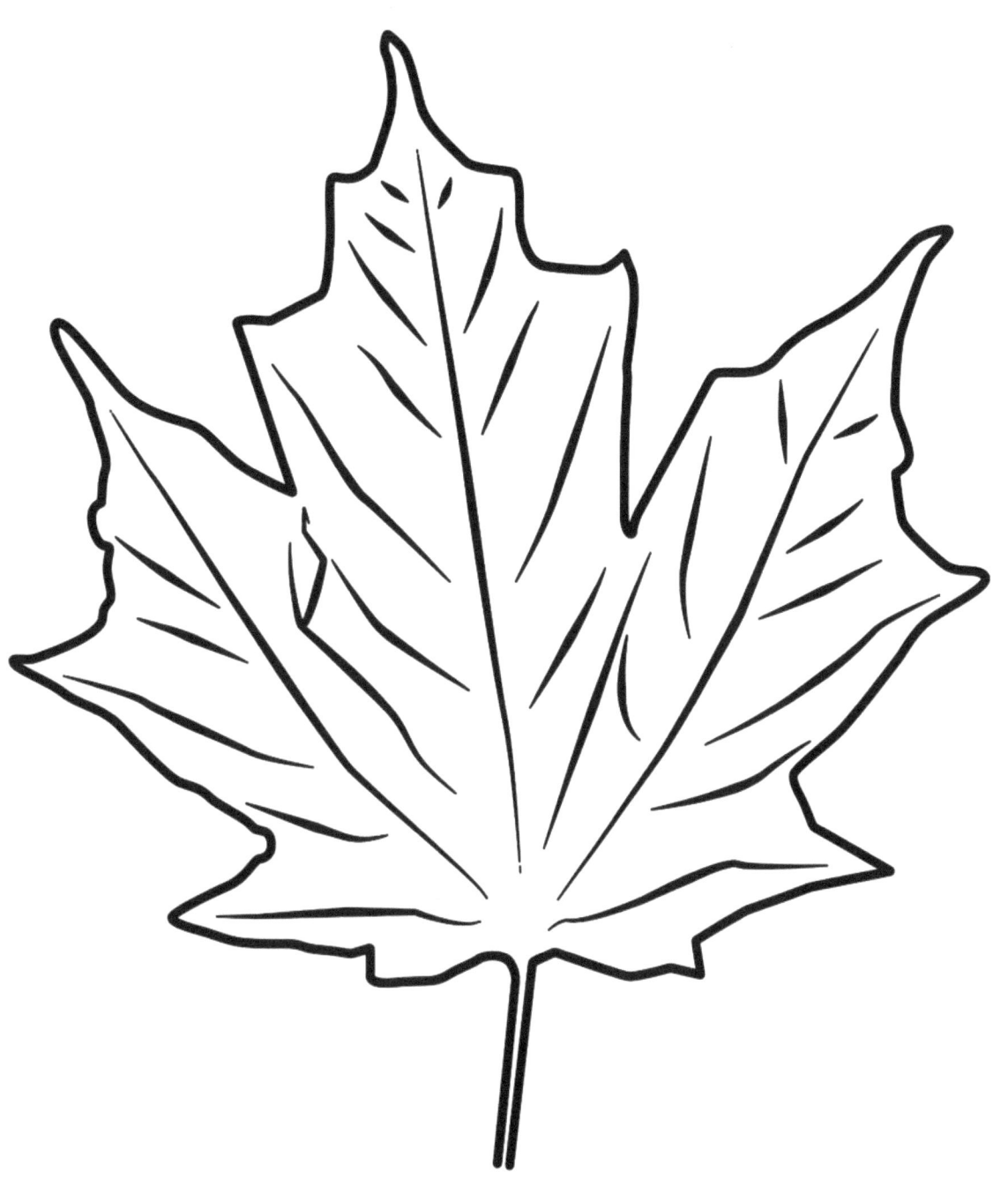

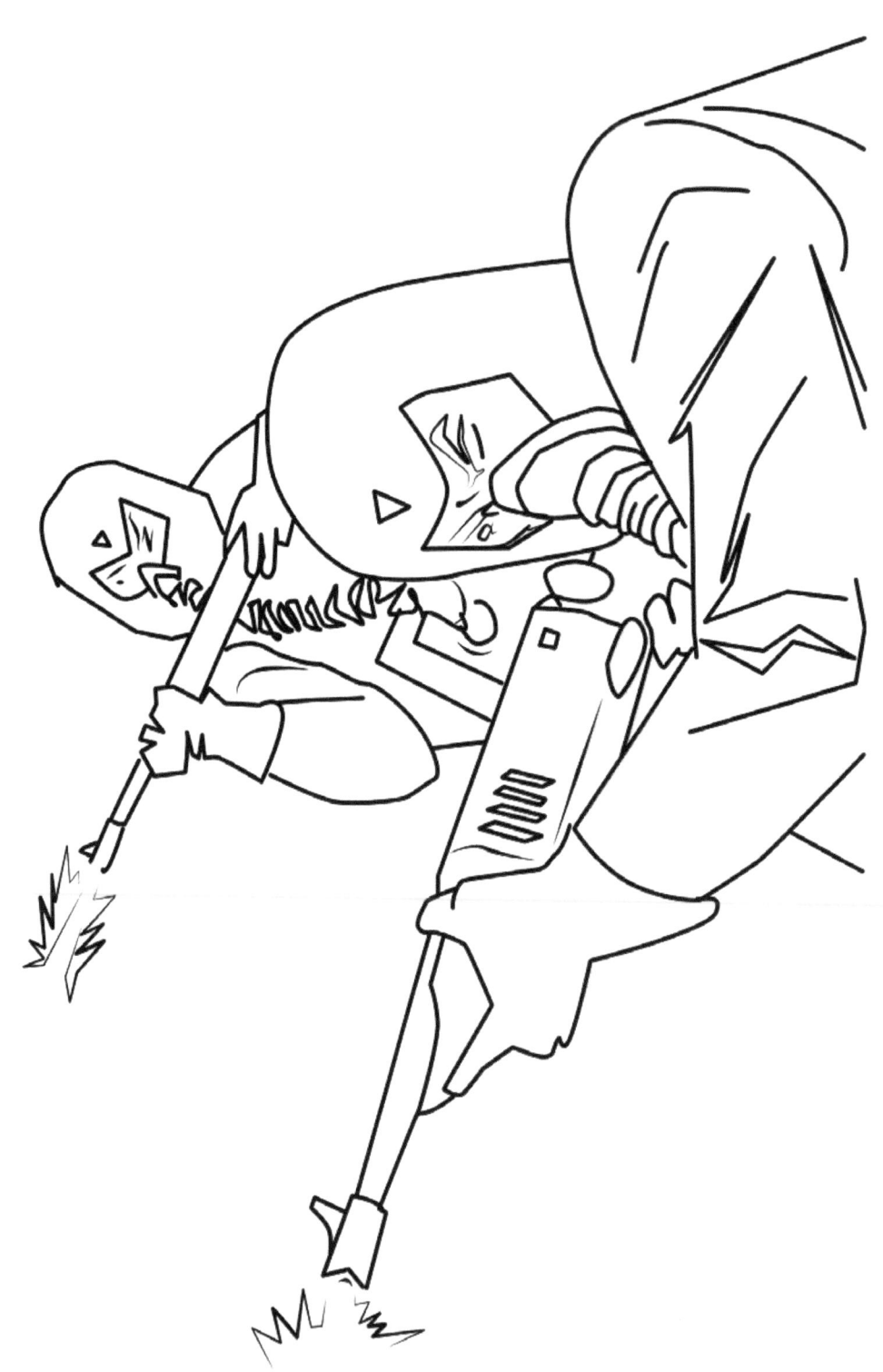

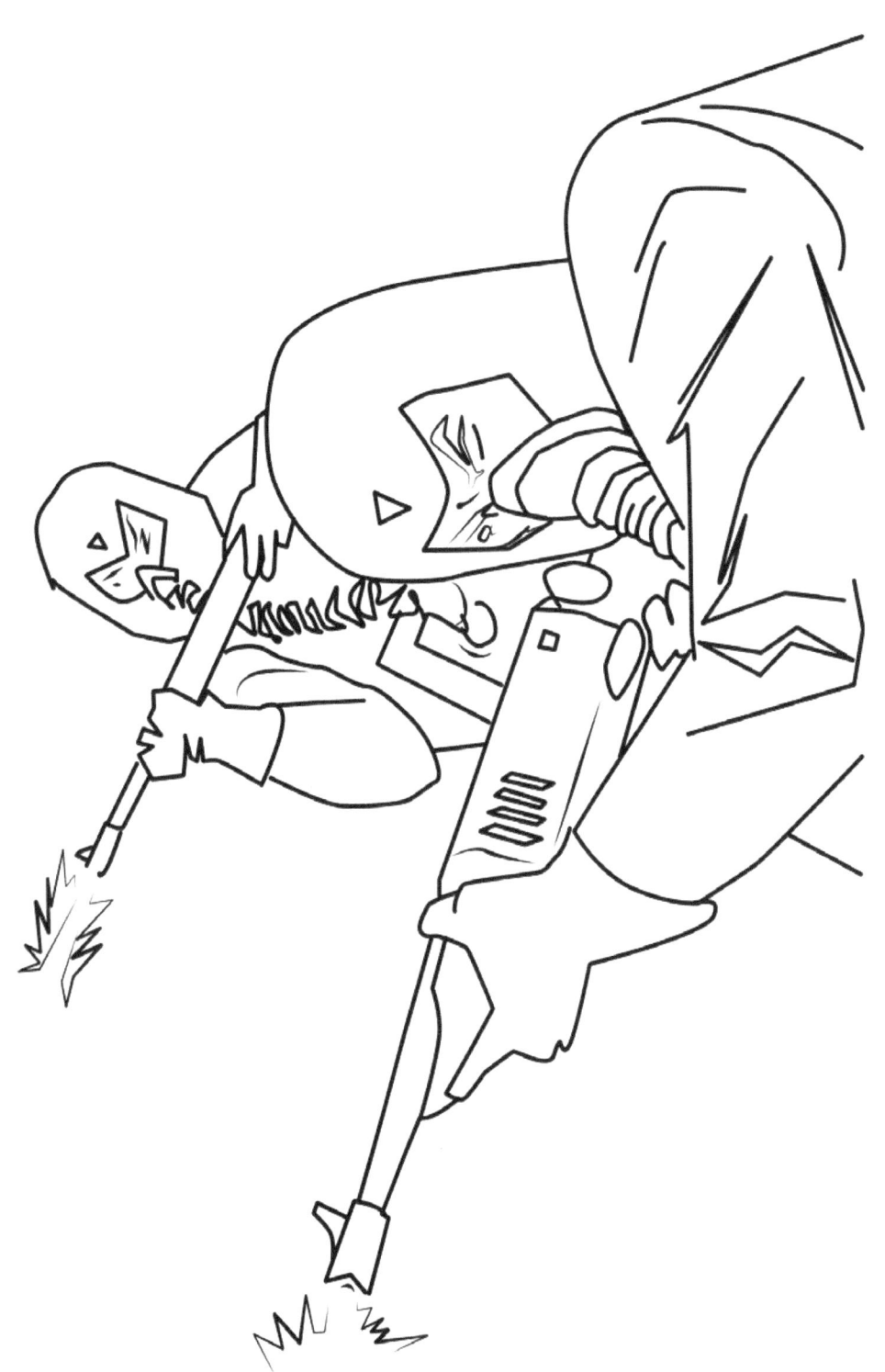

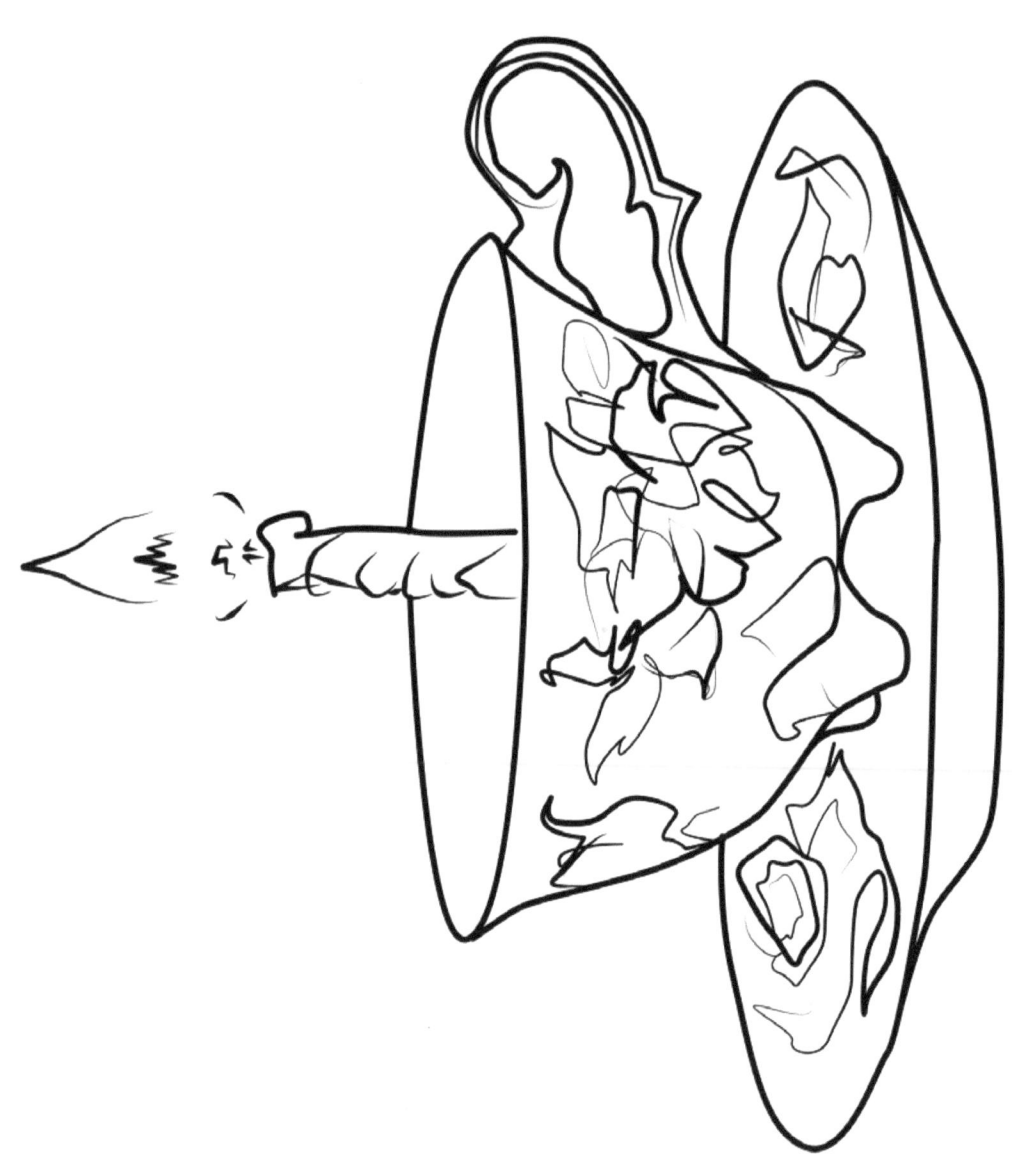

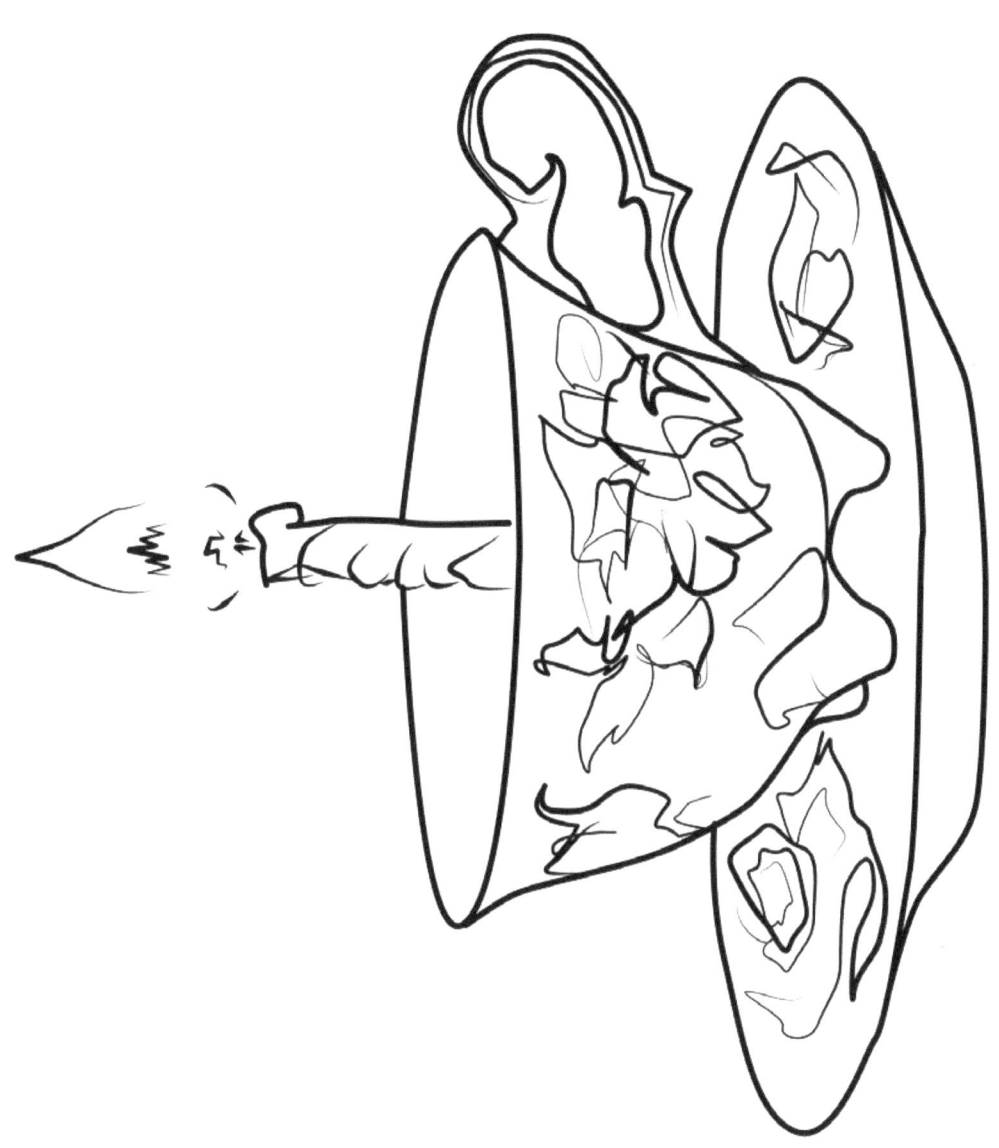

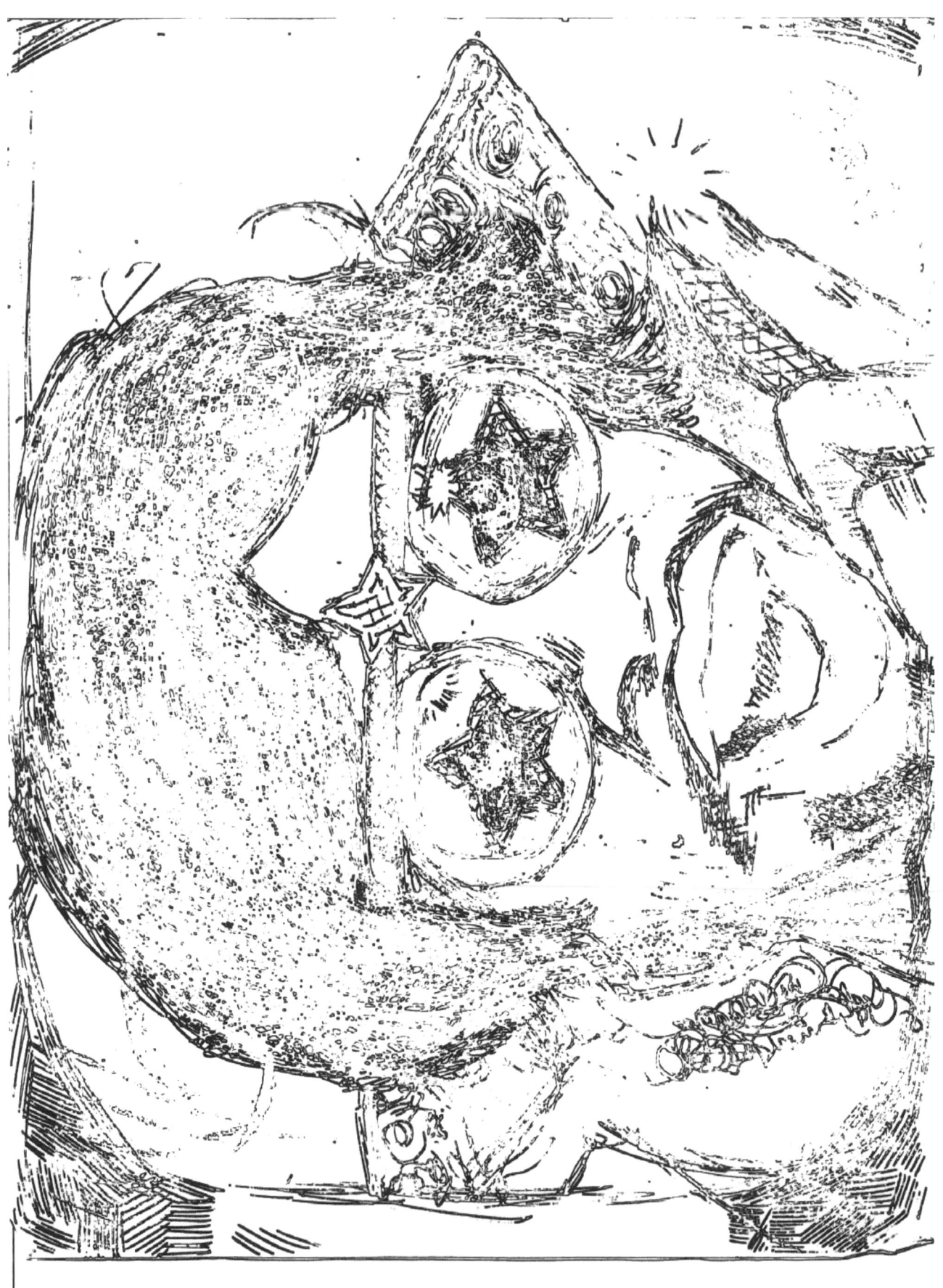

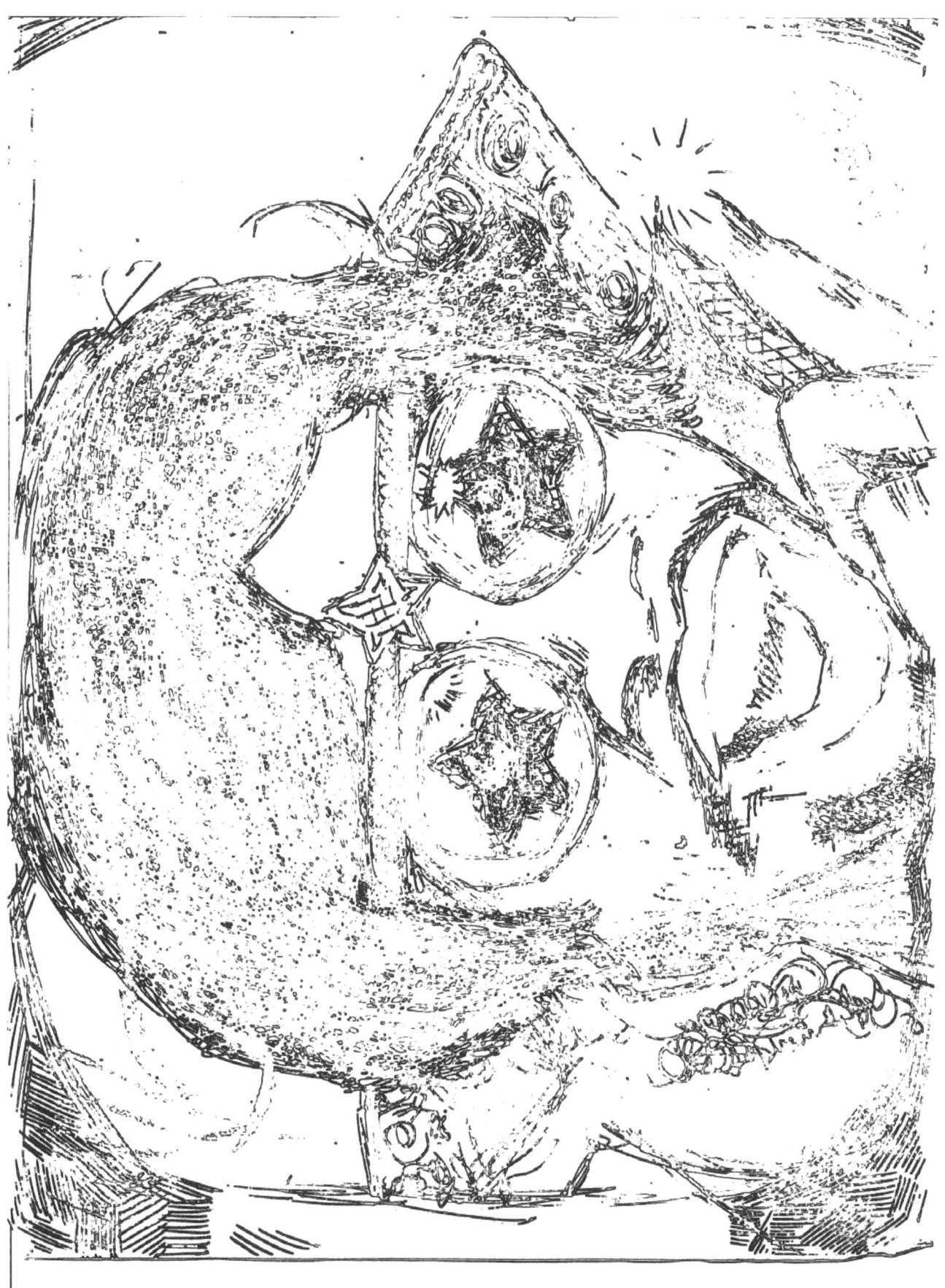

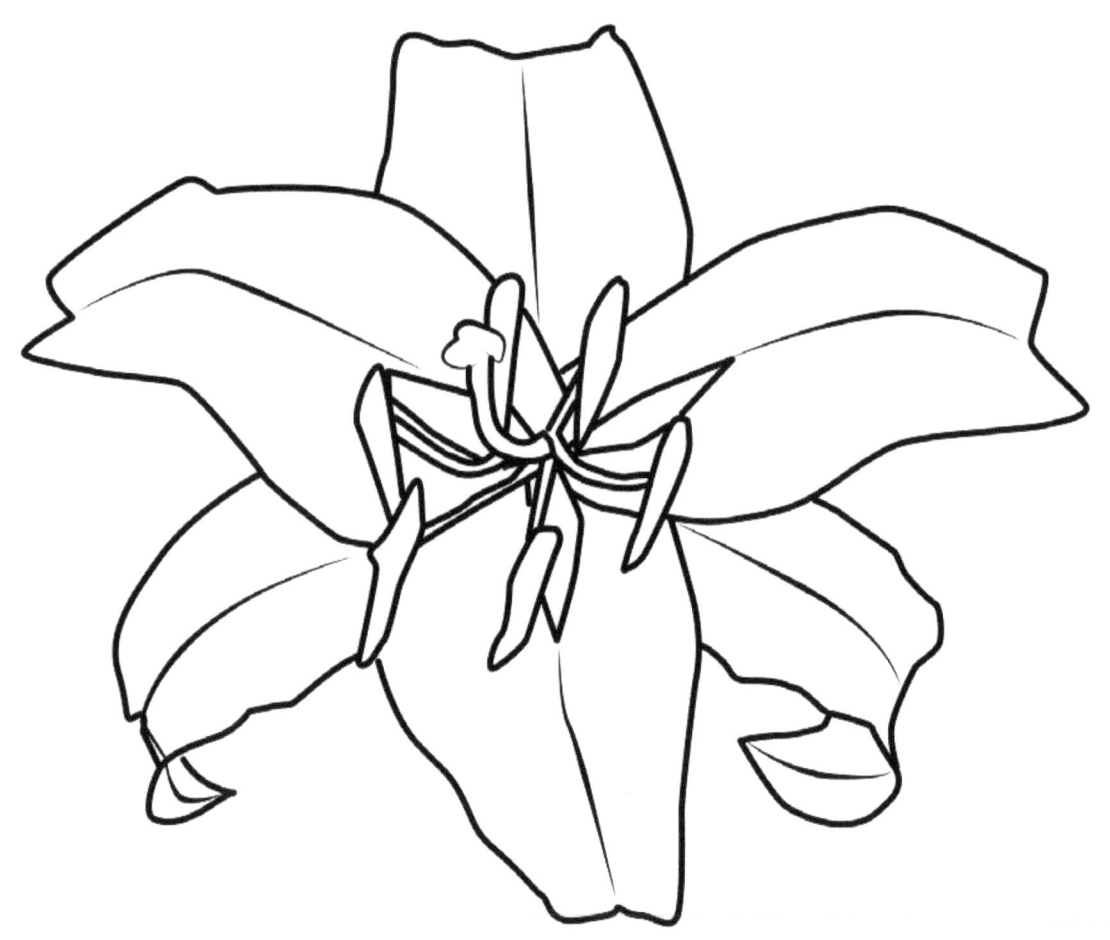

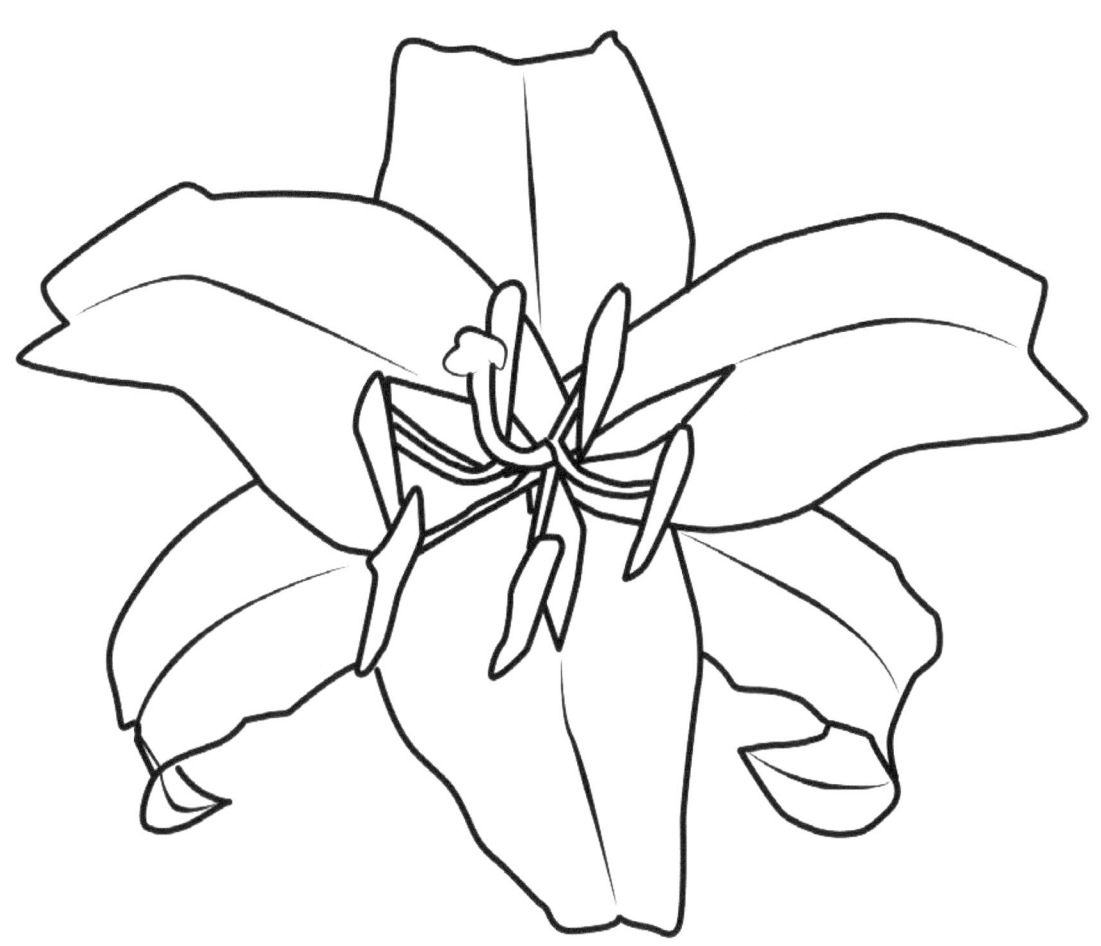

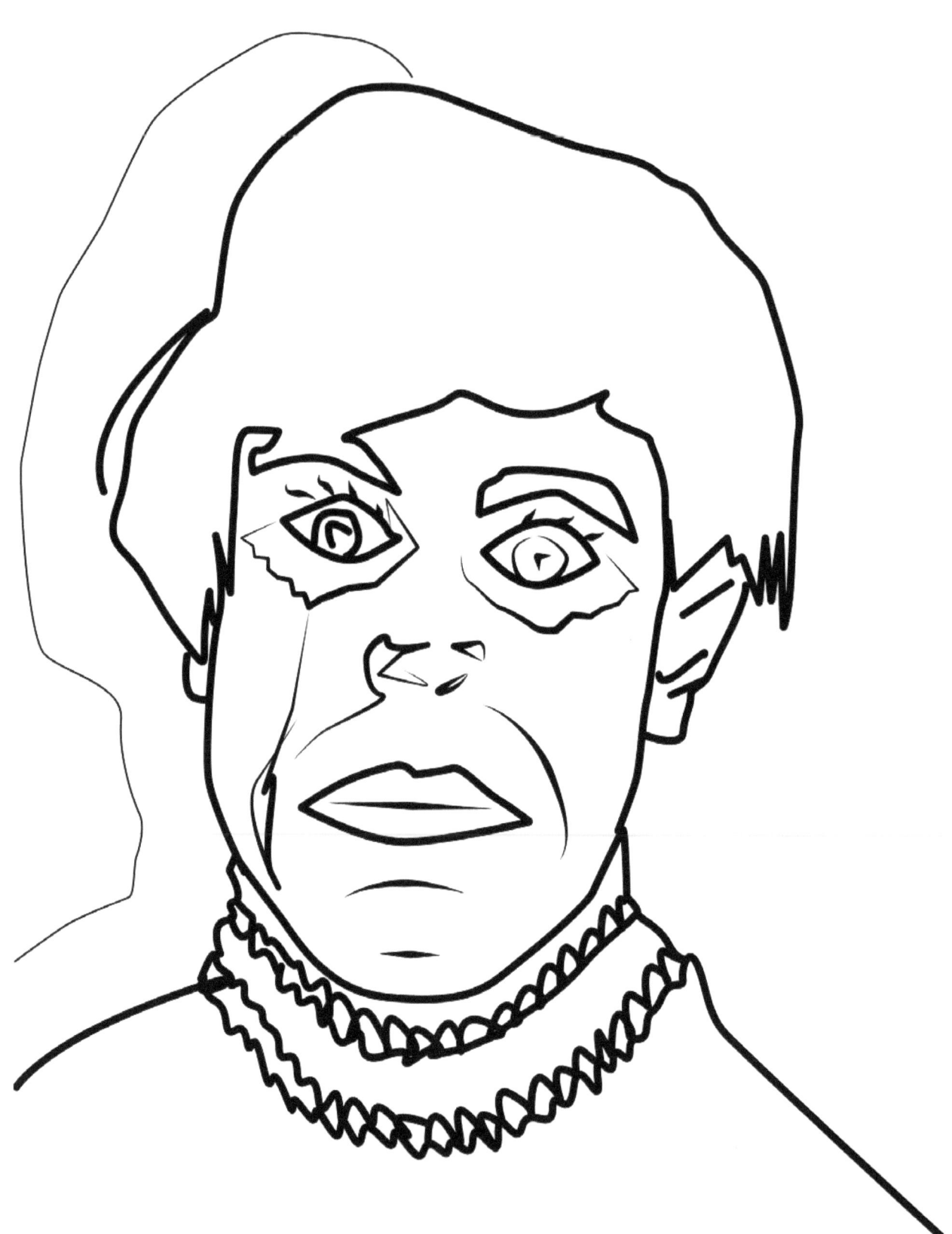

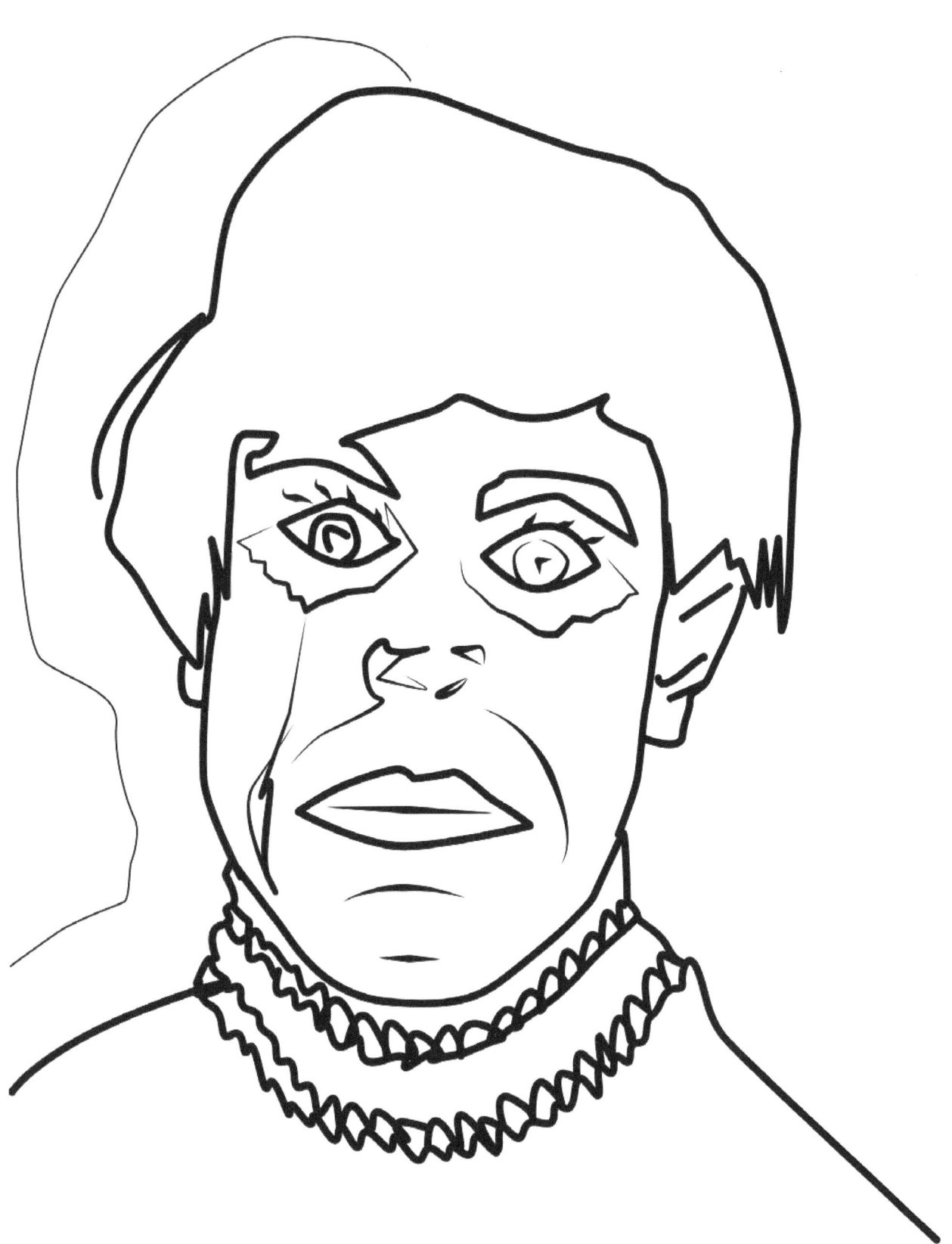

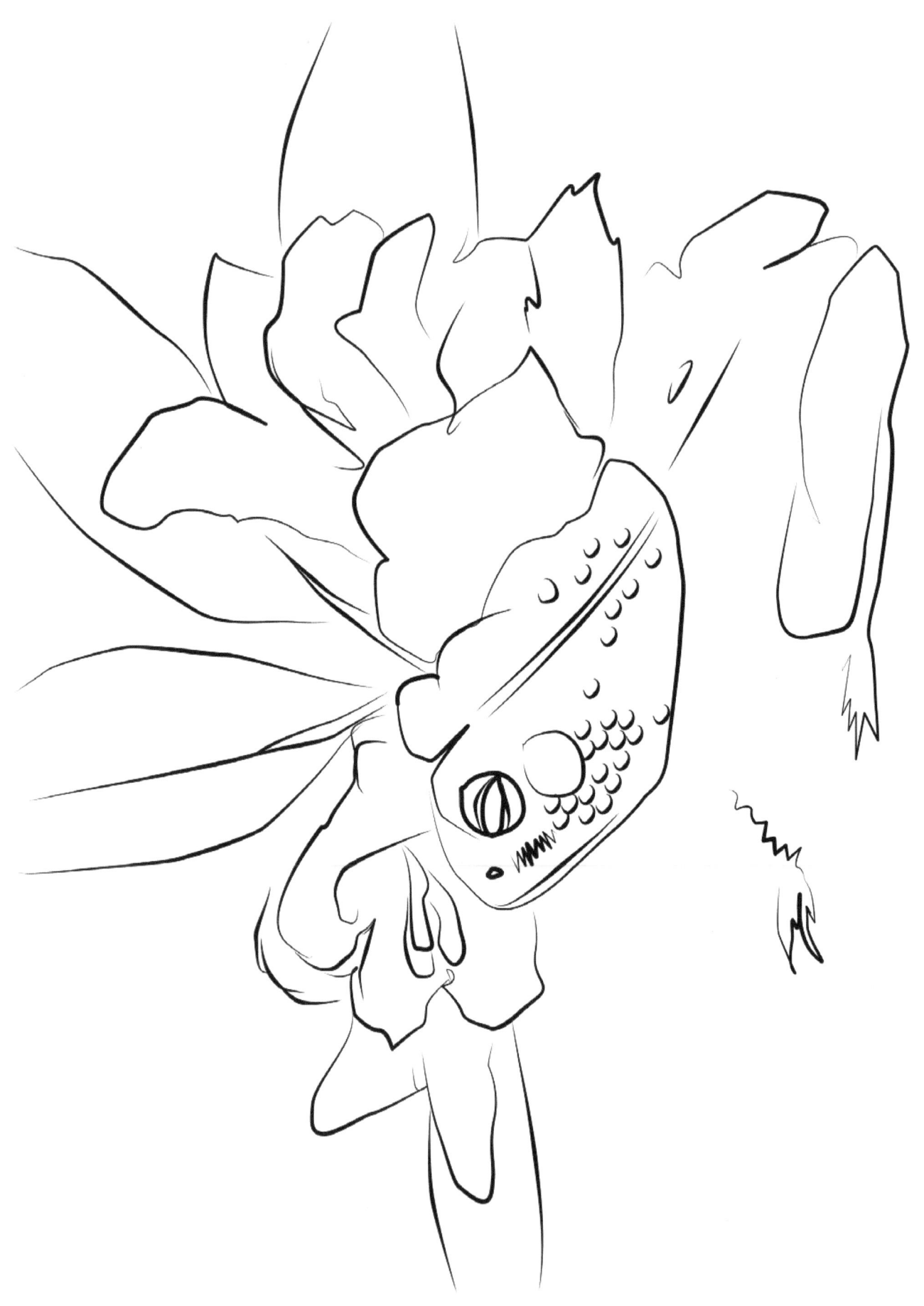

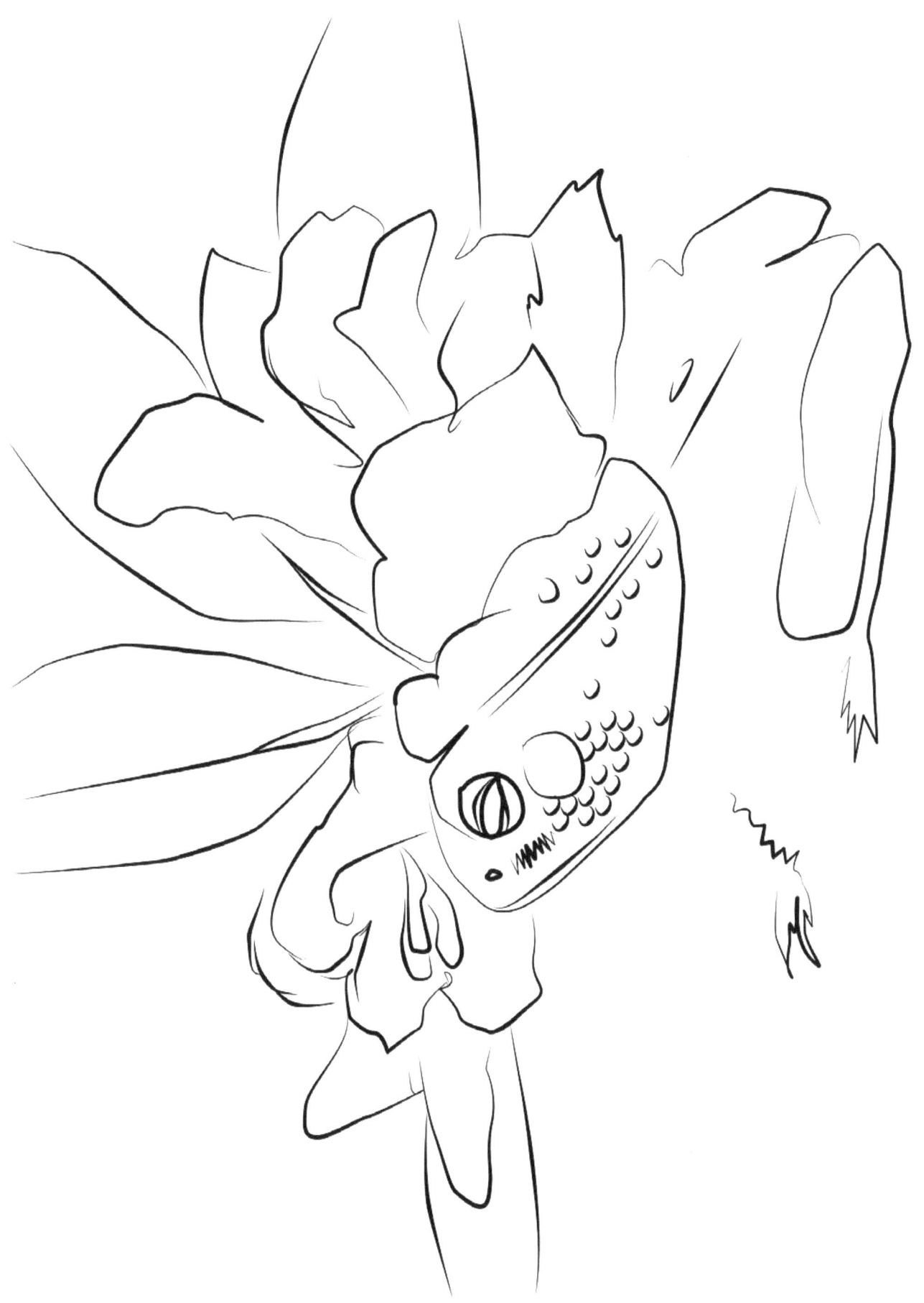

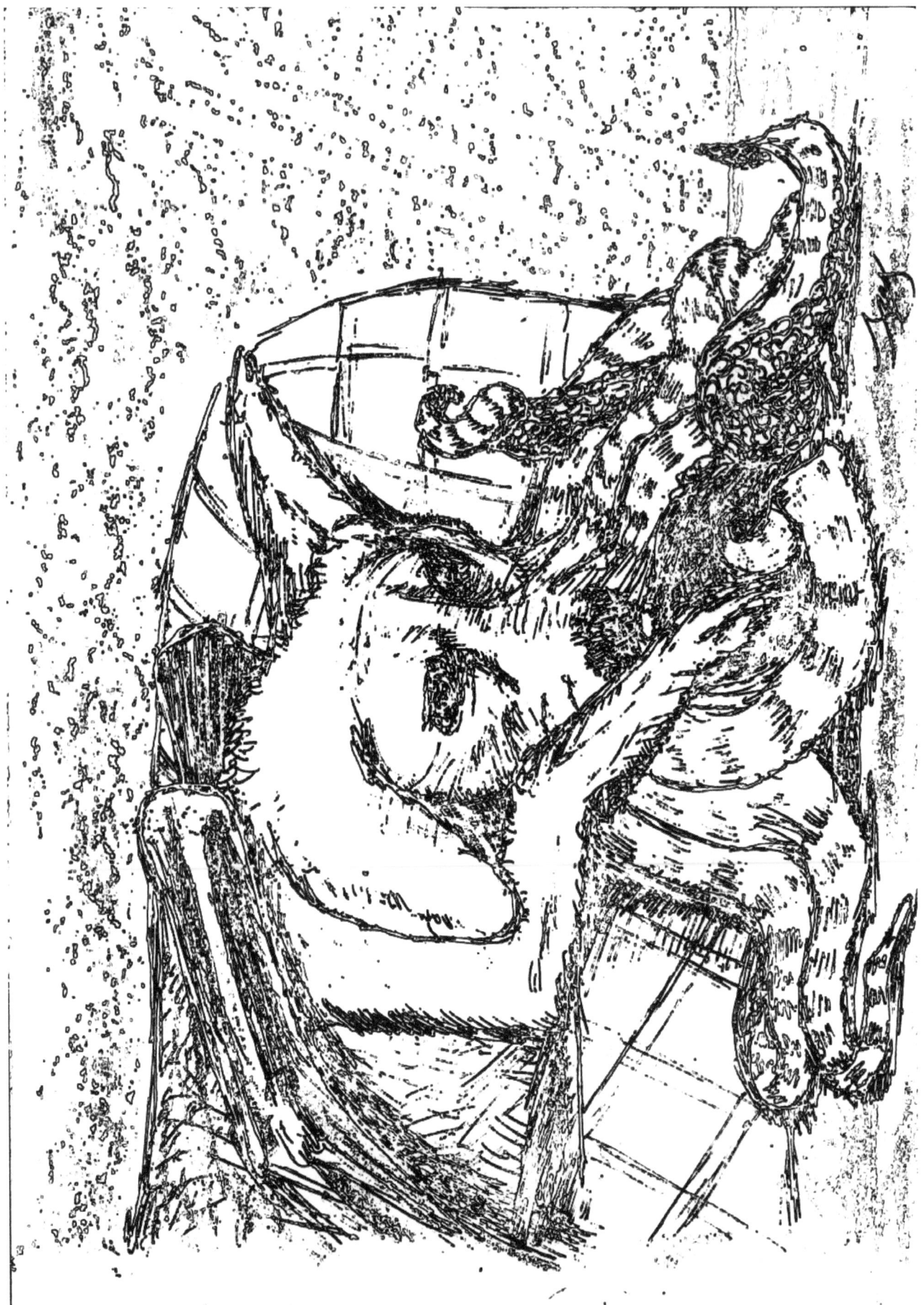

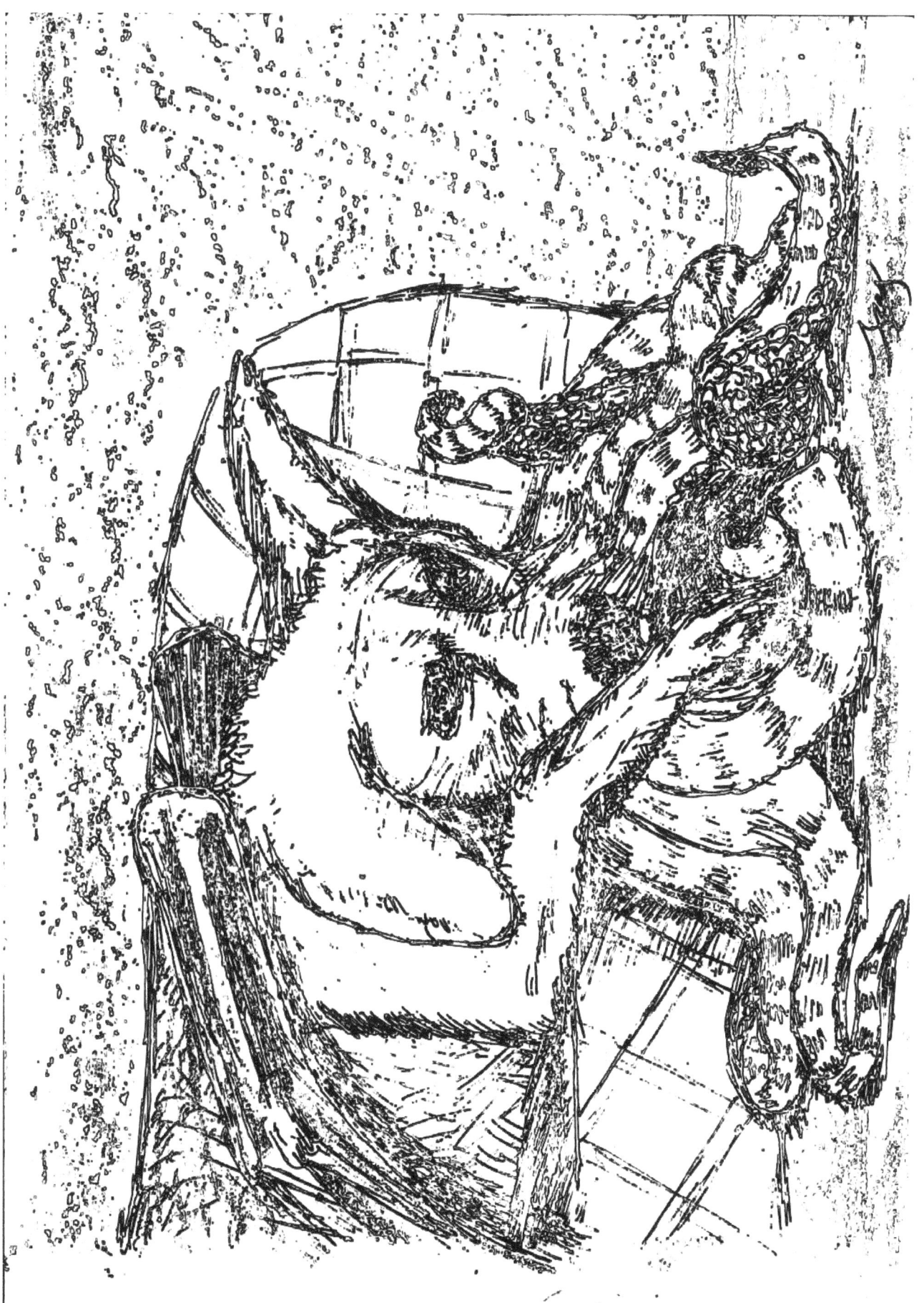

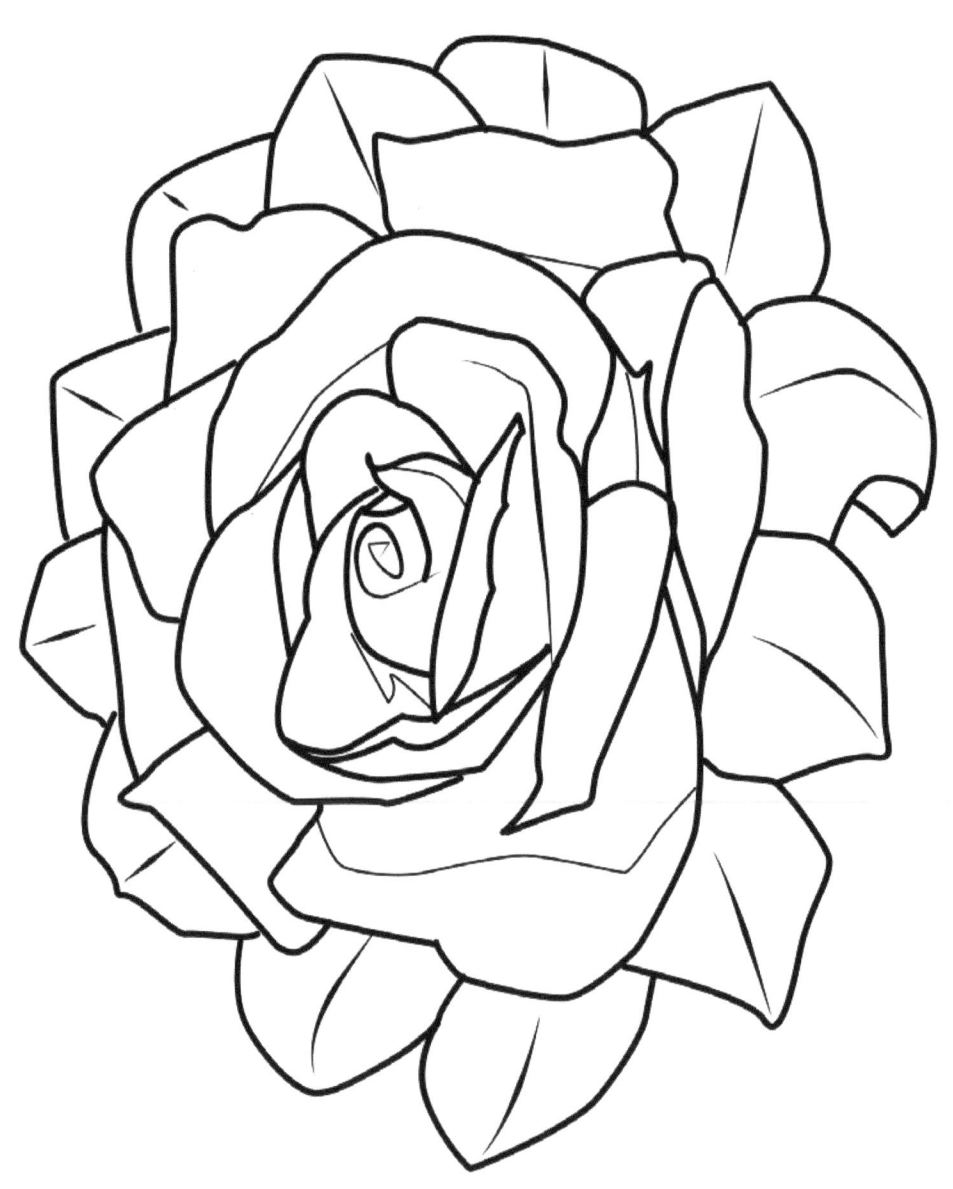

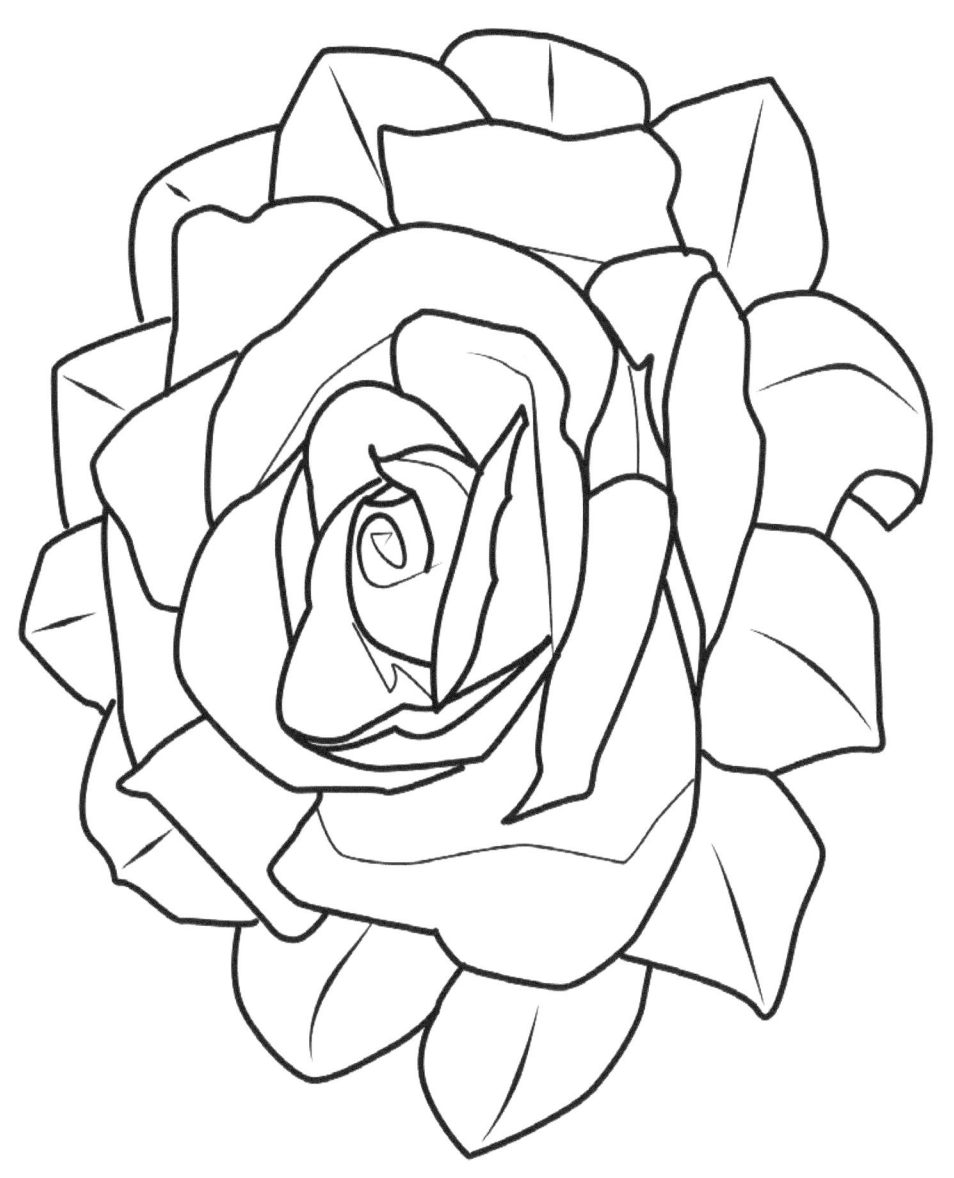

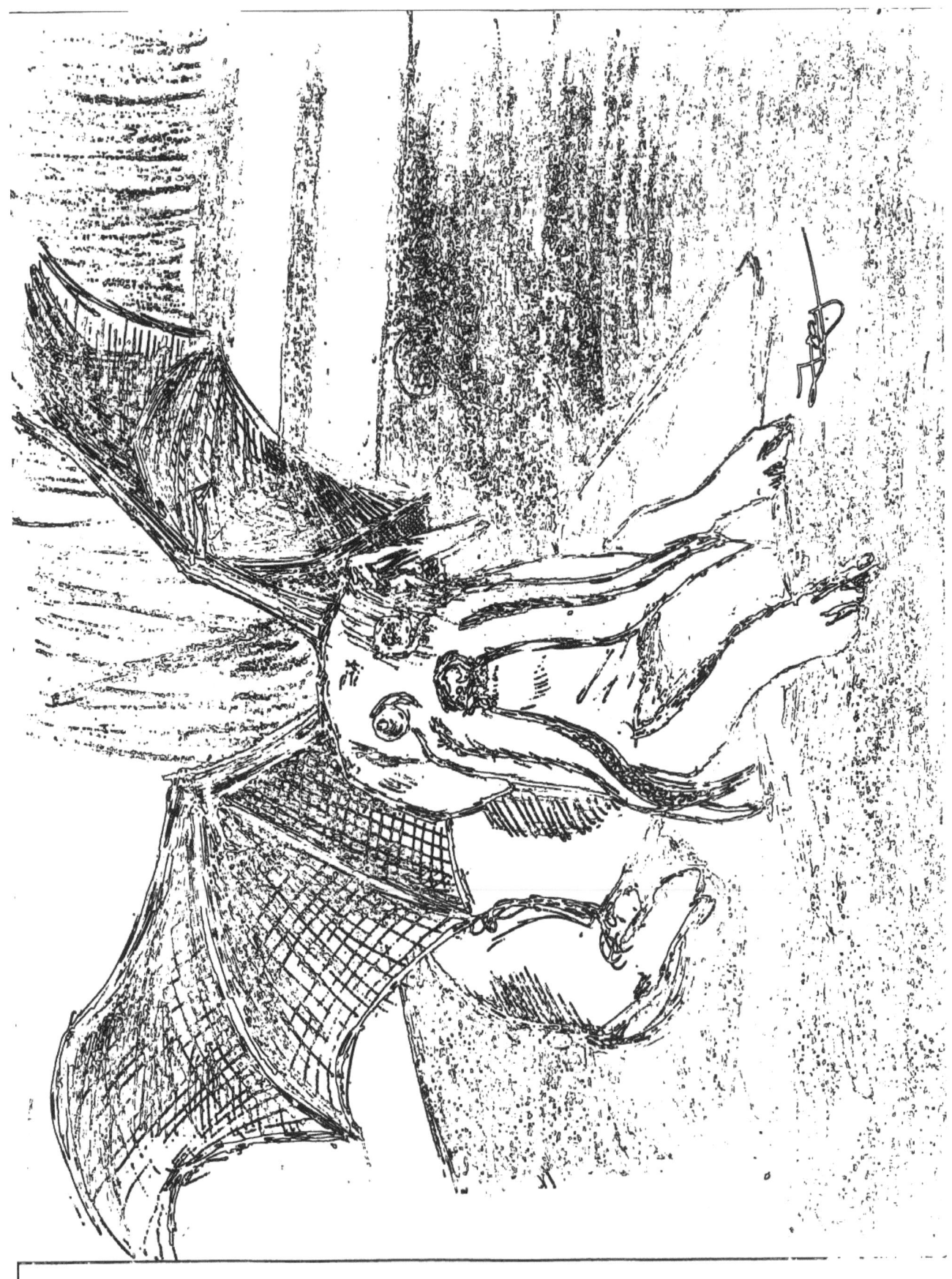

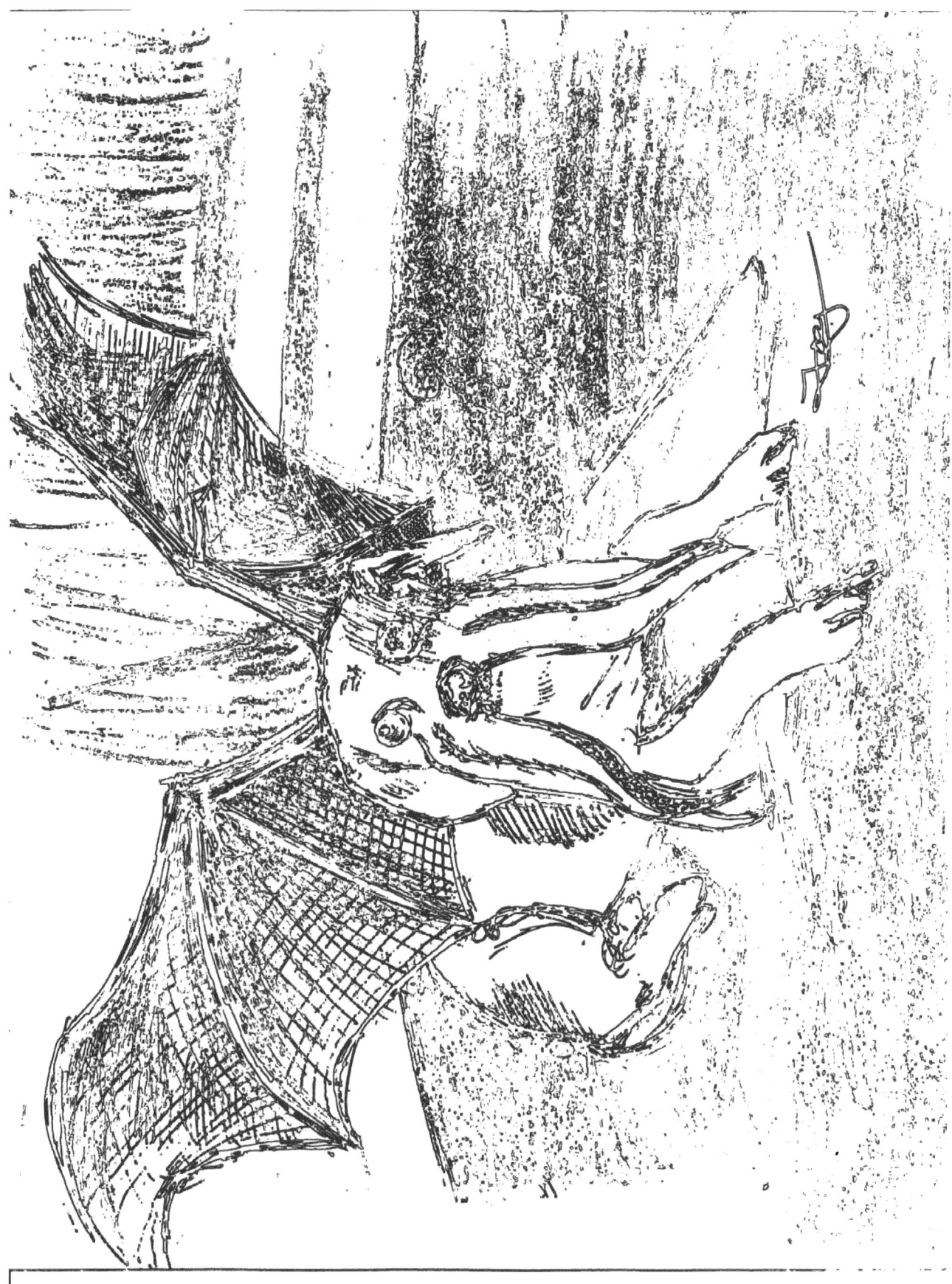

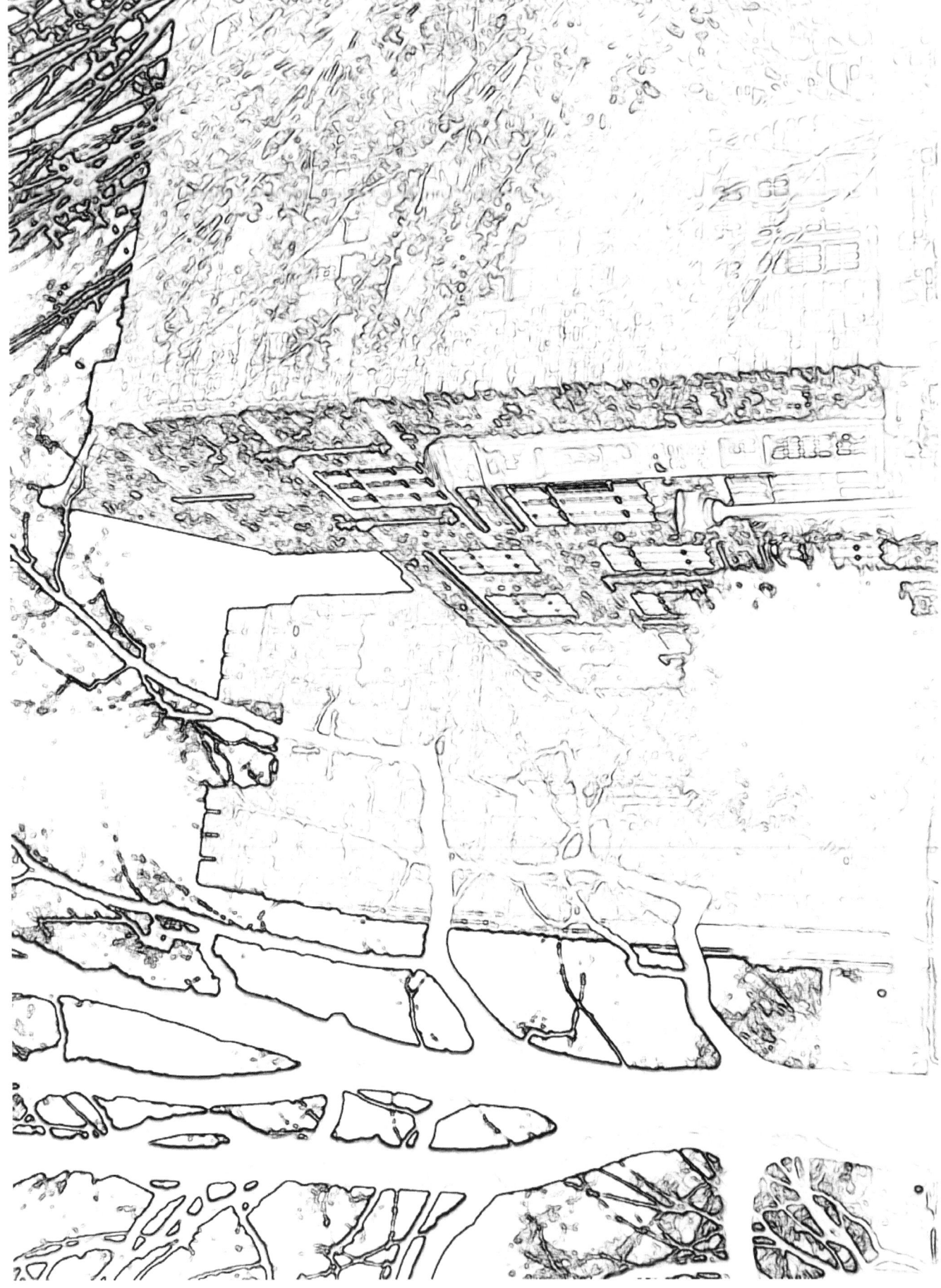

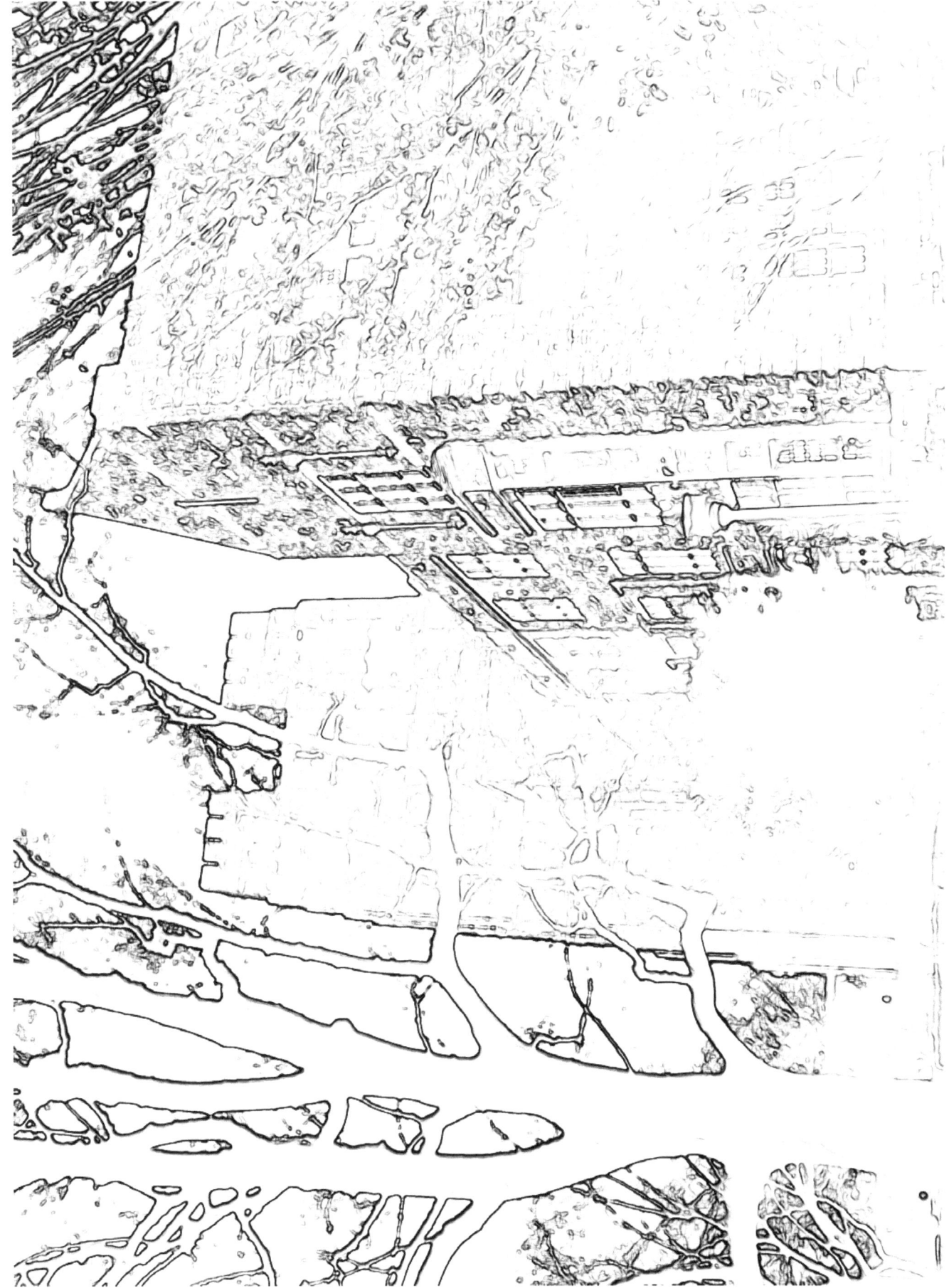

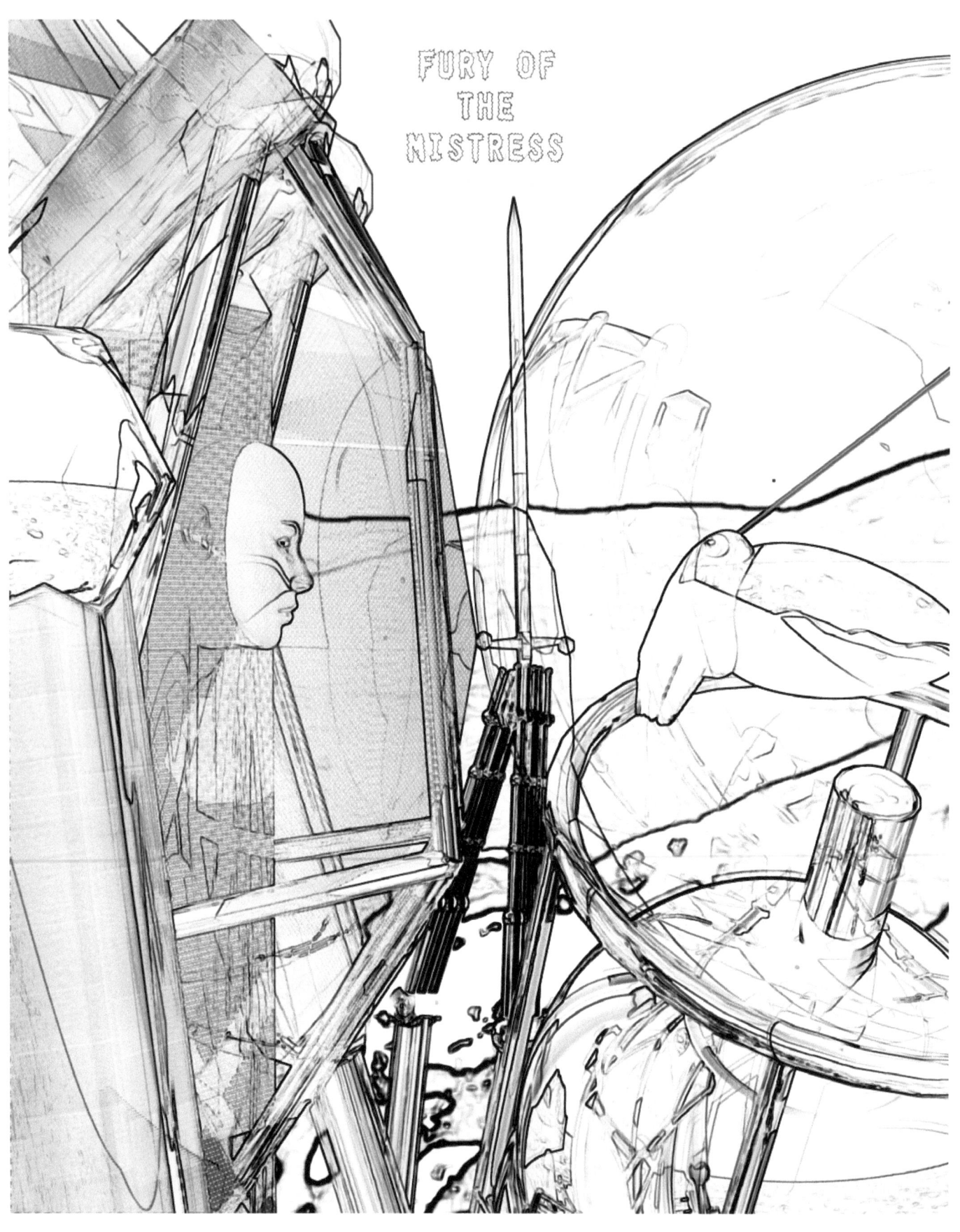

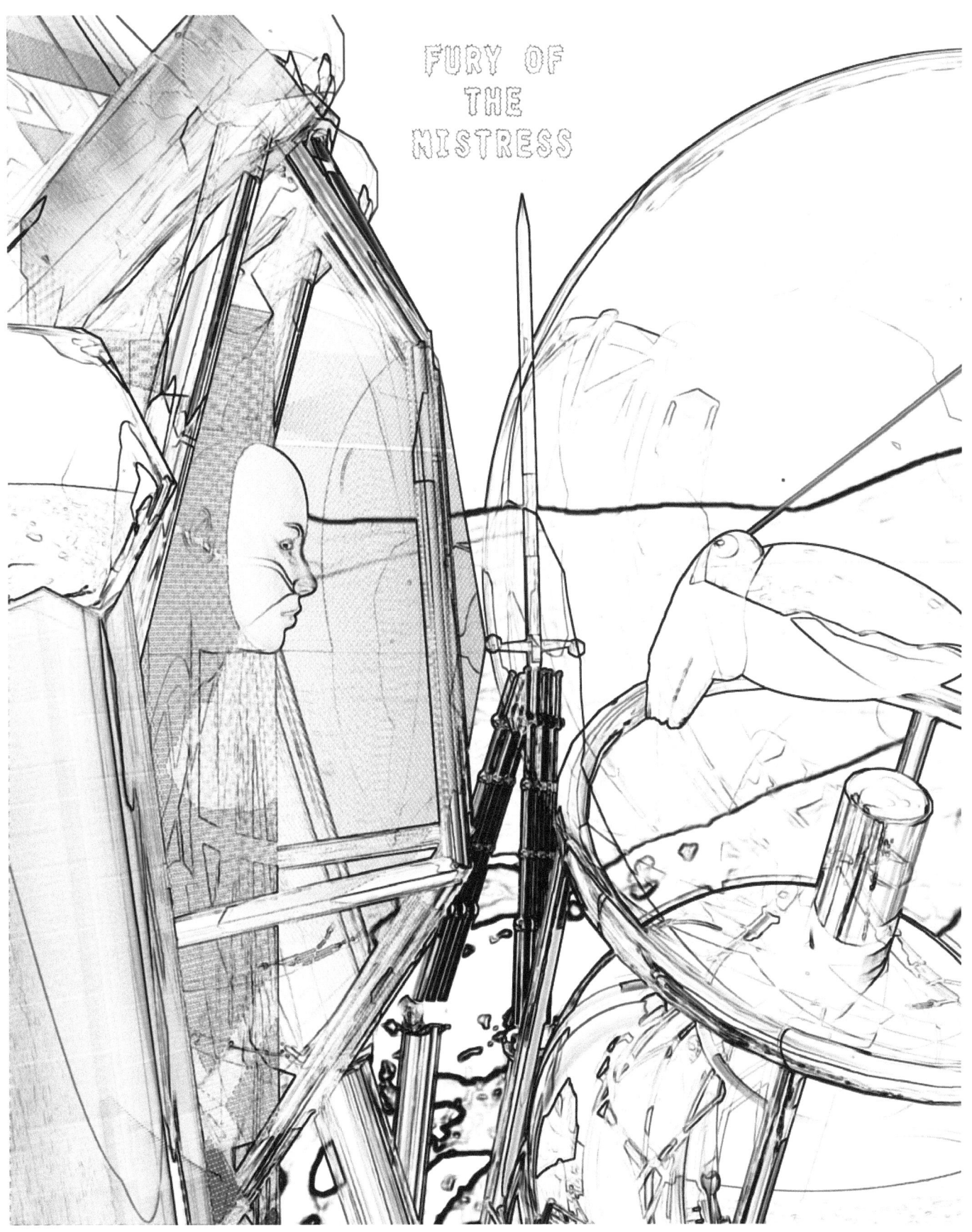

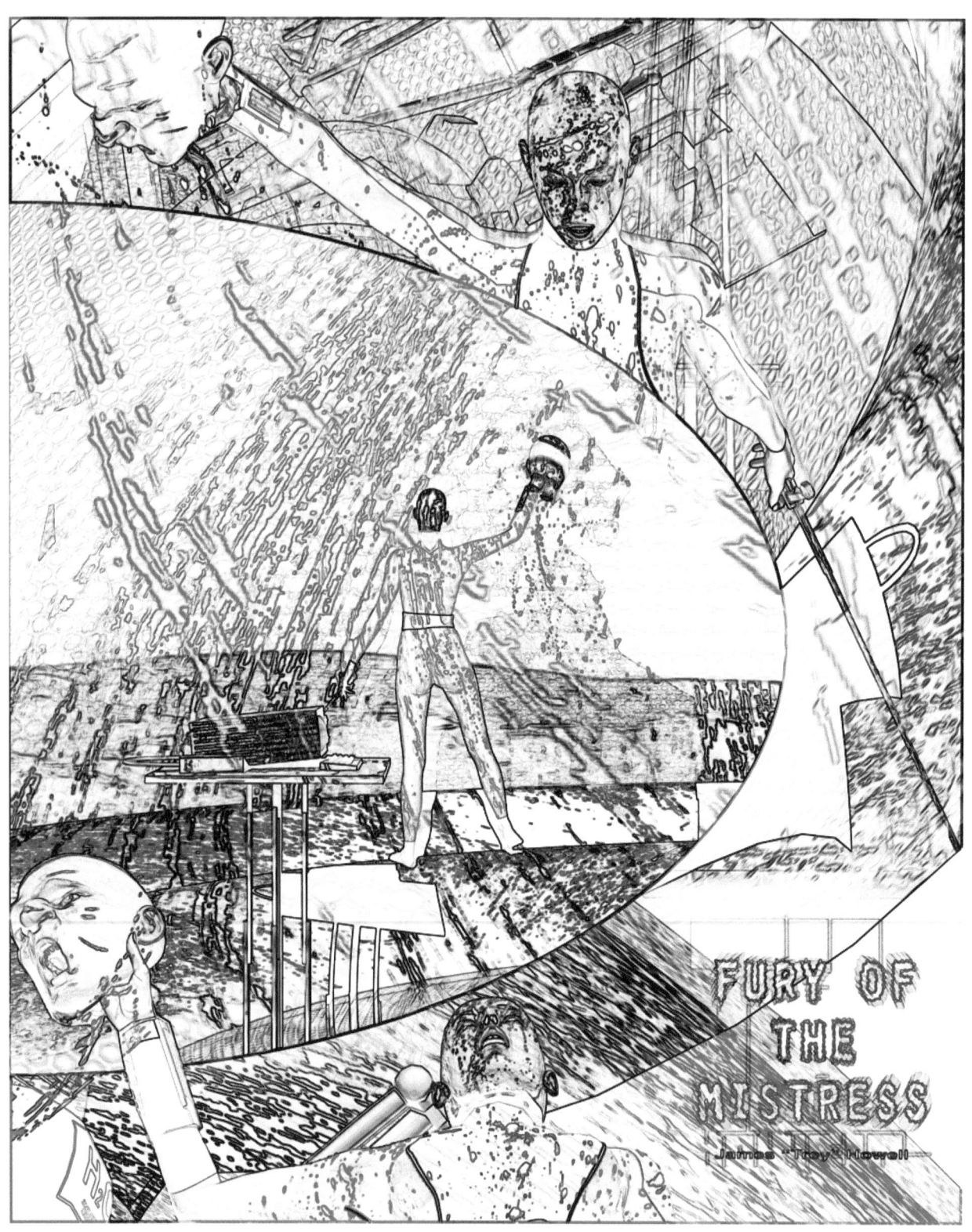

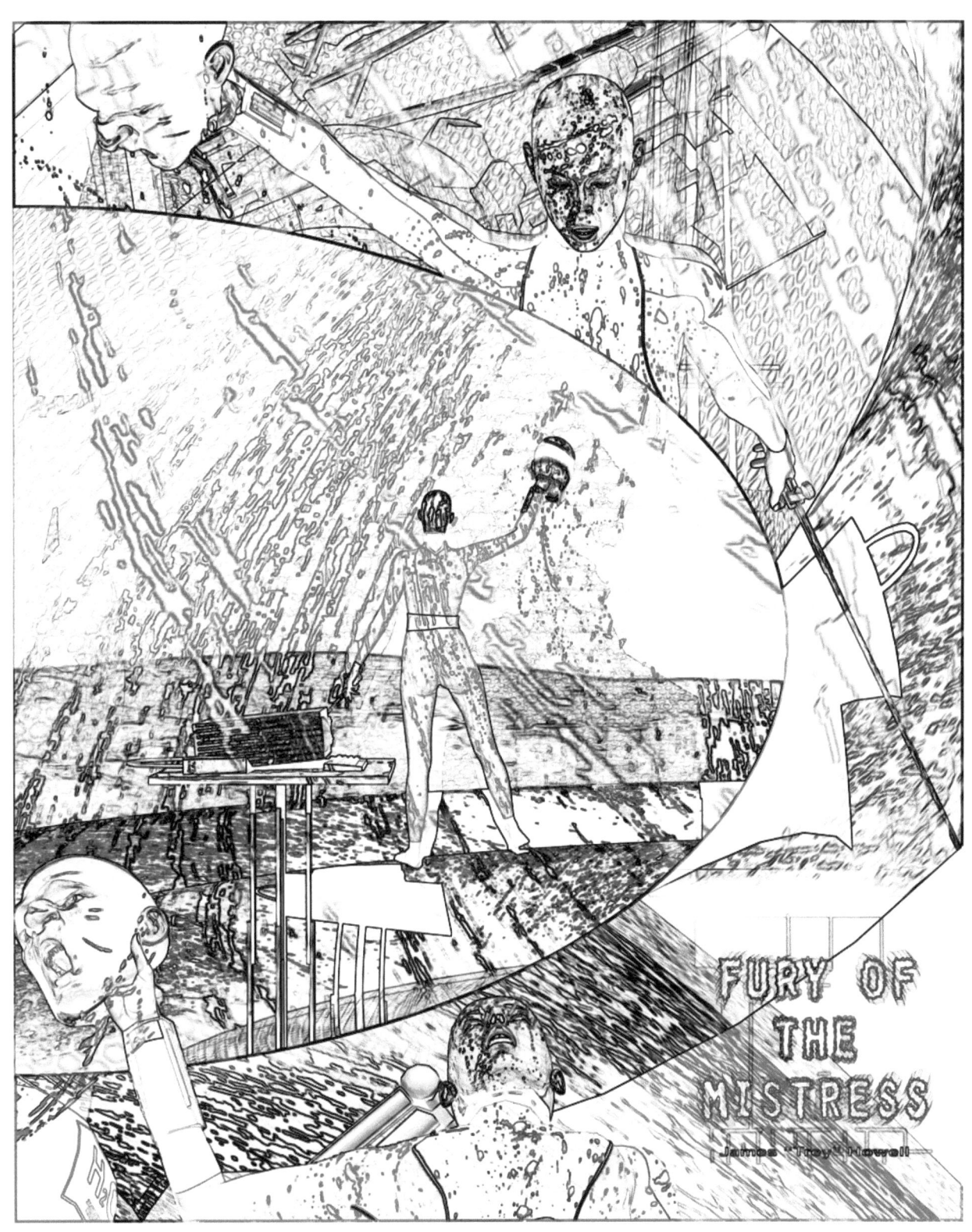

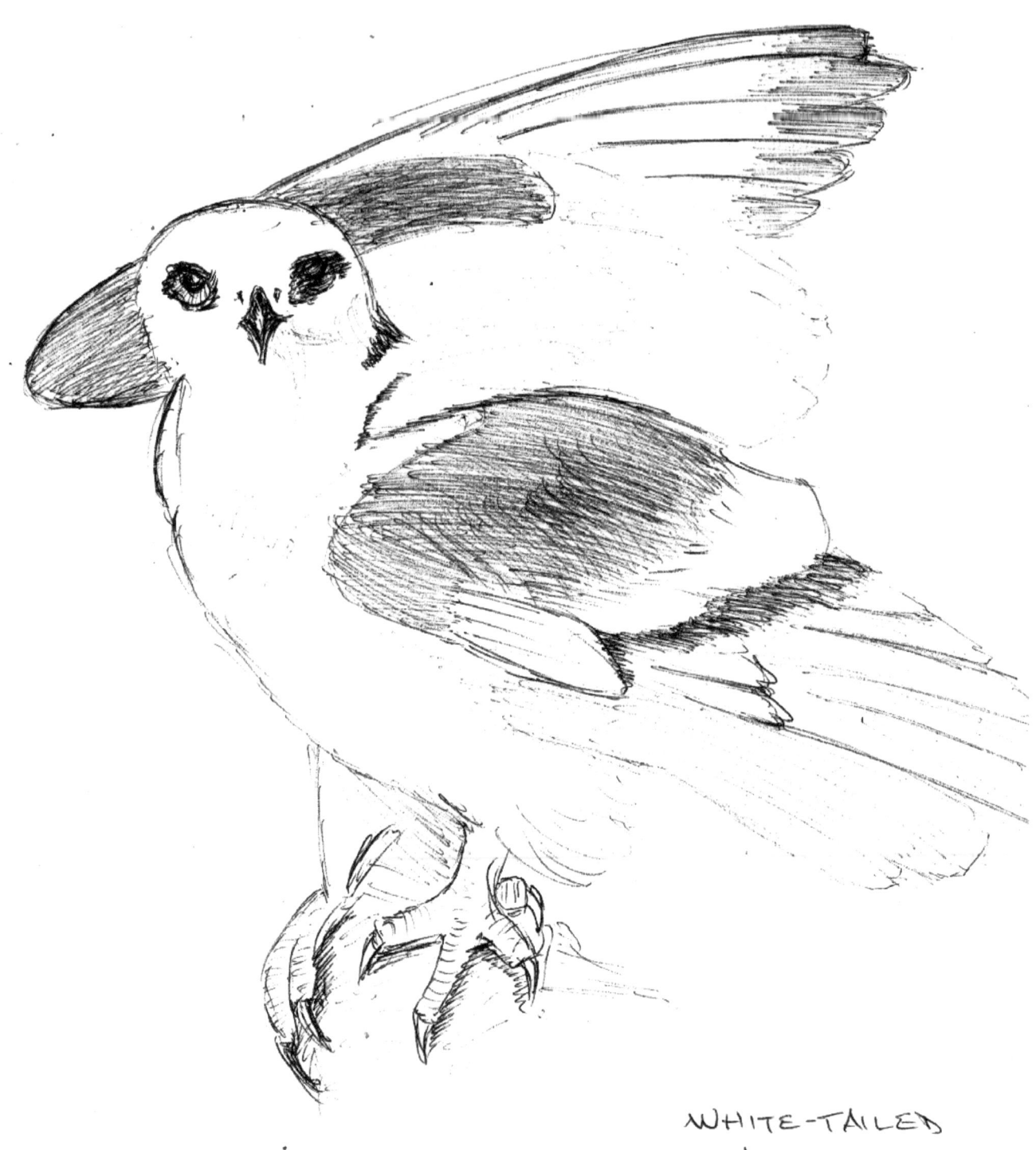

WHITE-TAILED KITE

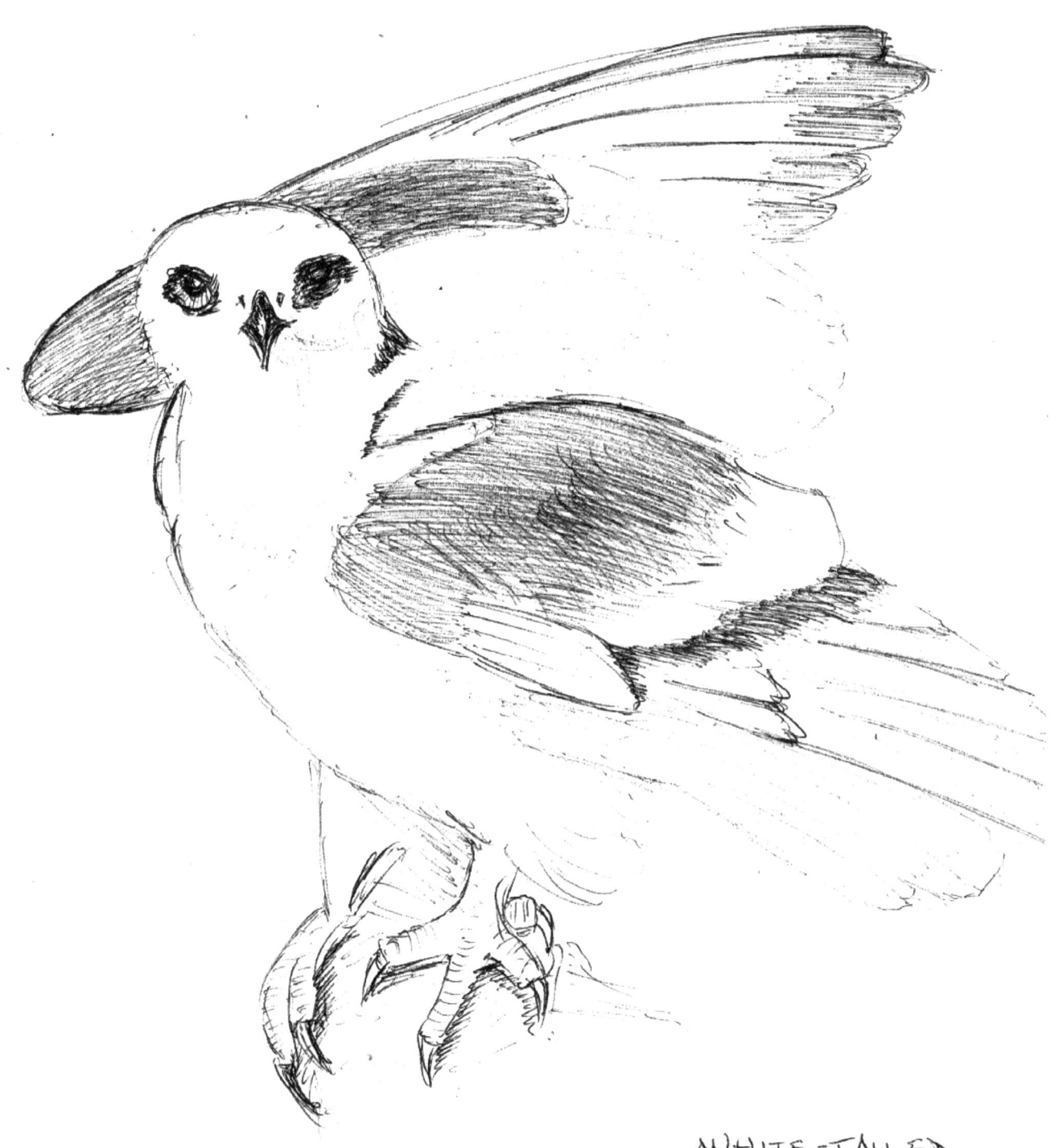

WHITE-TAILED KITE

Grey

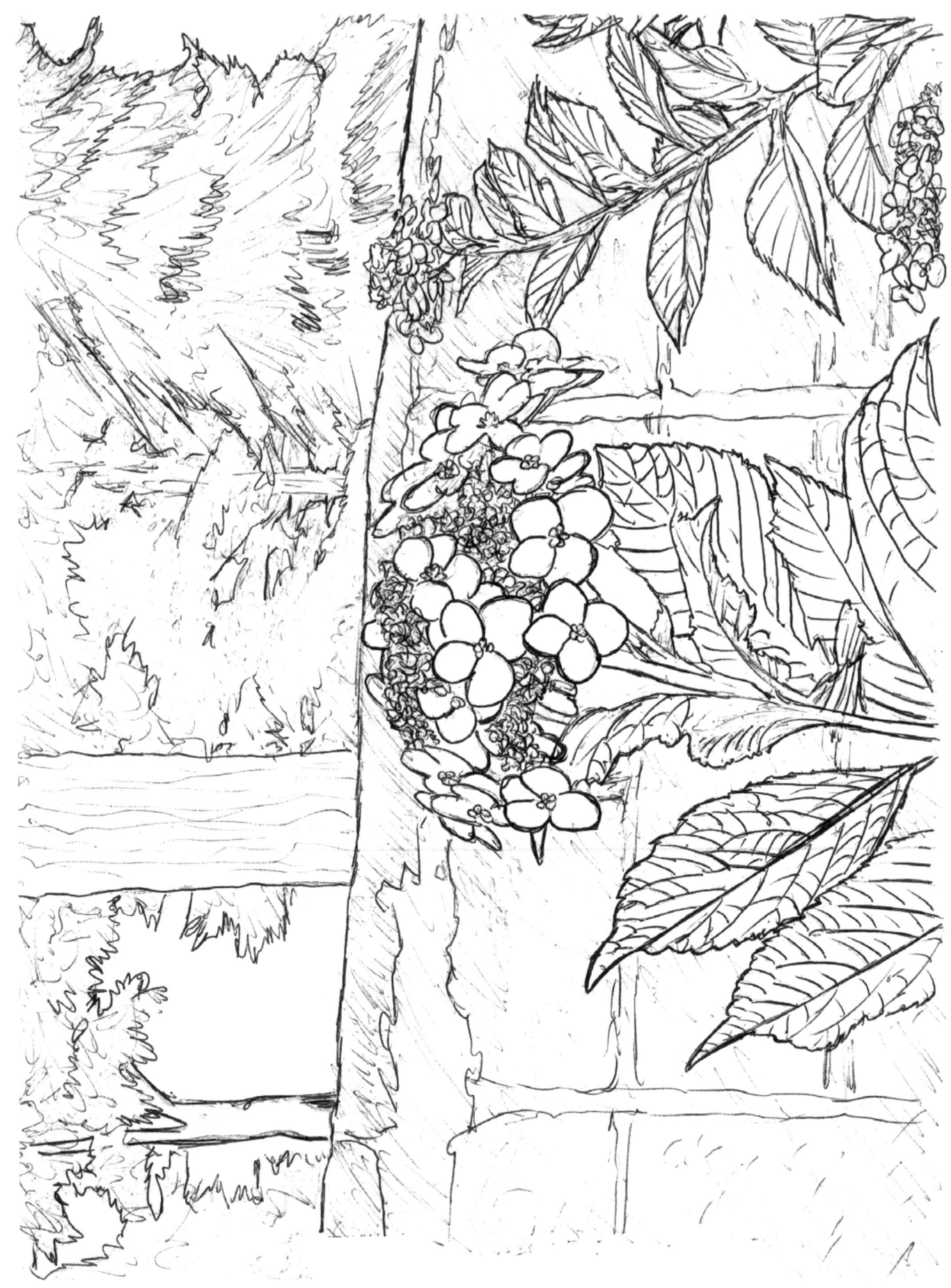

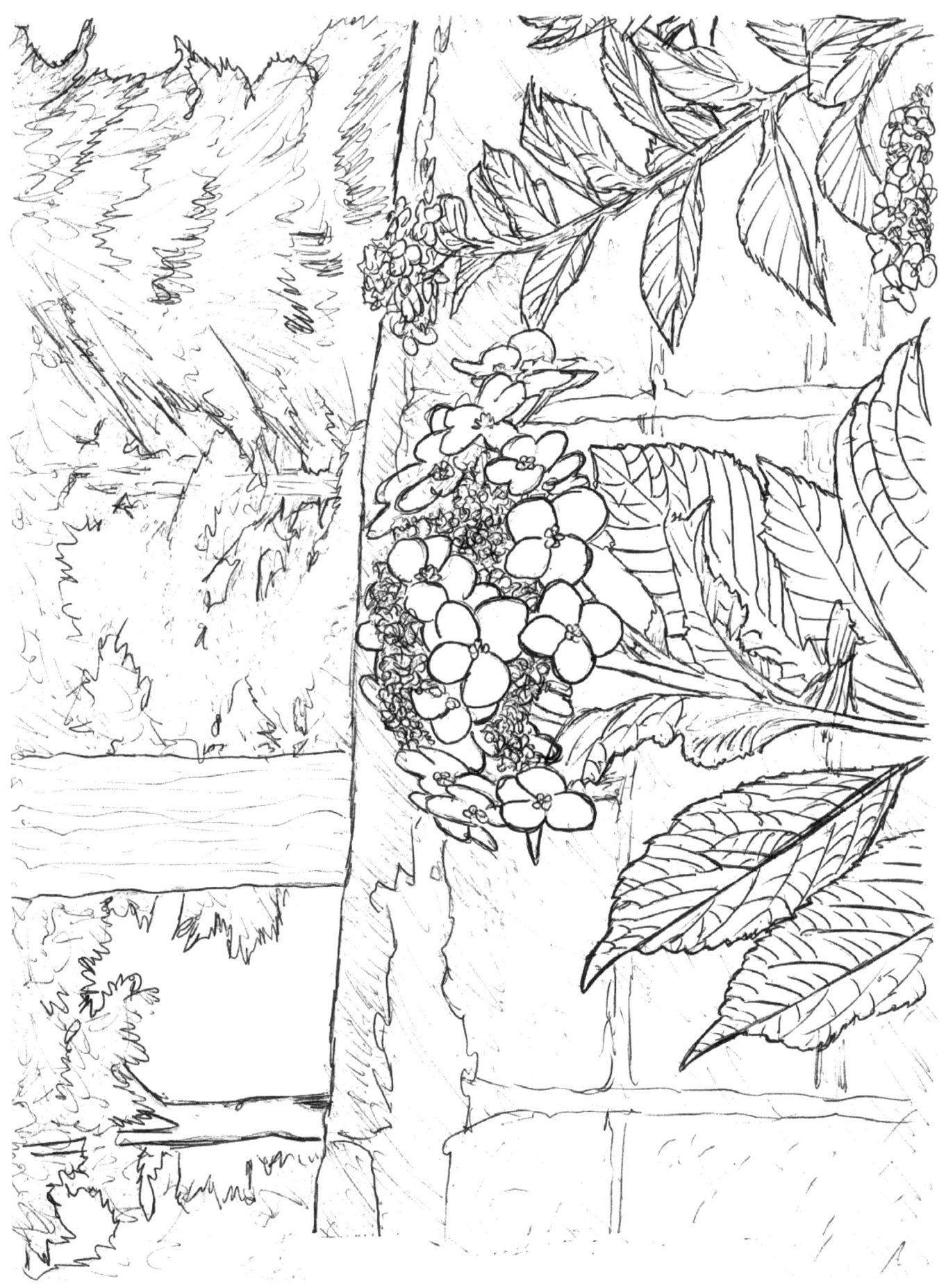

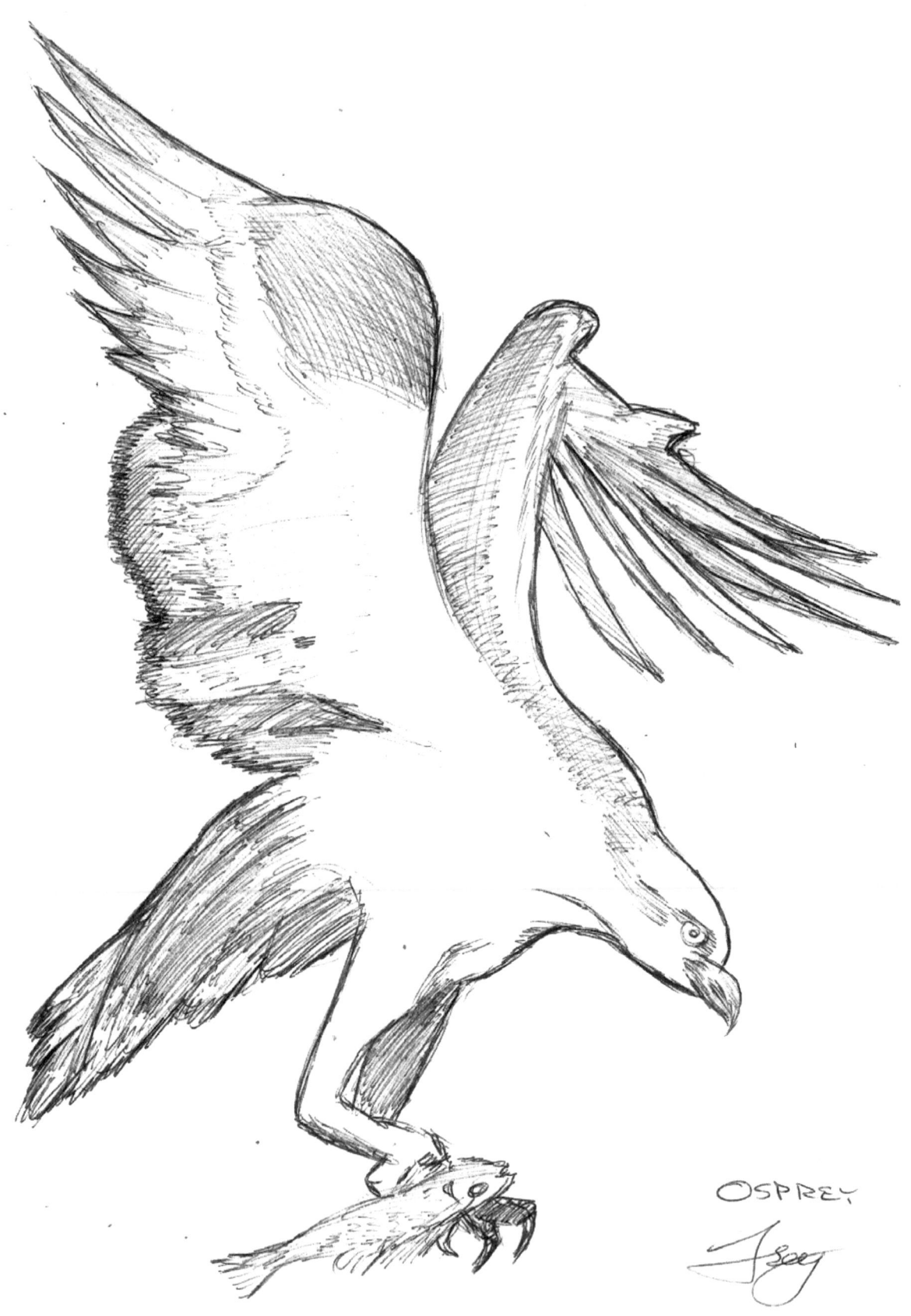

OSPREY

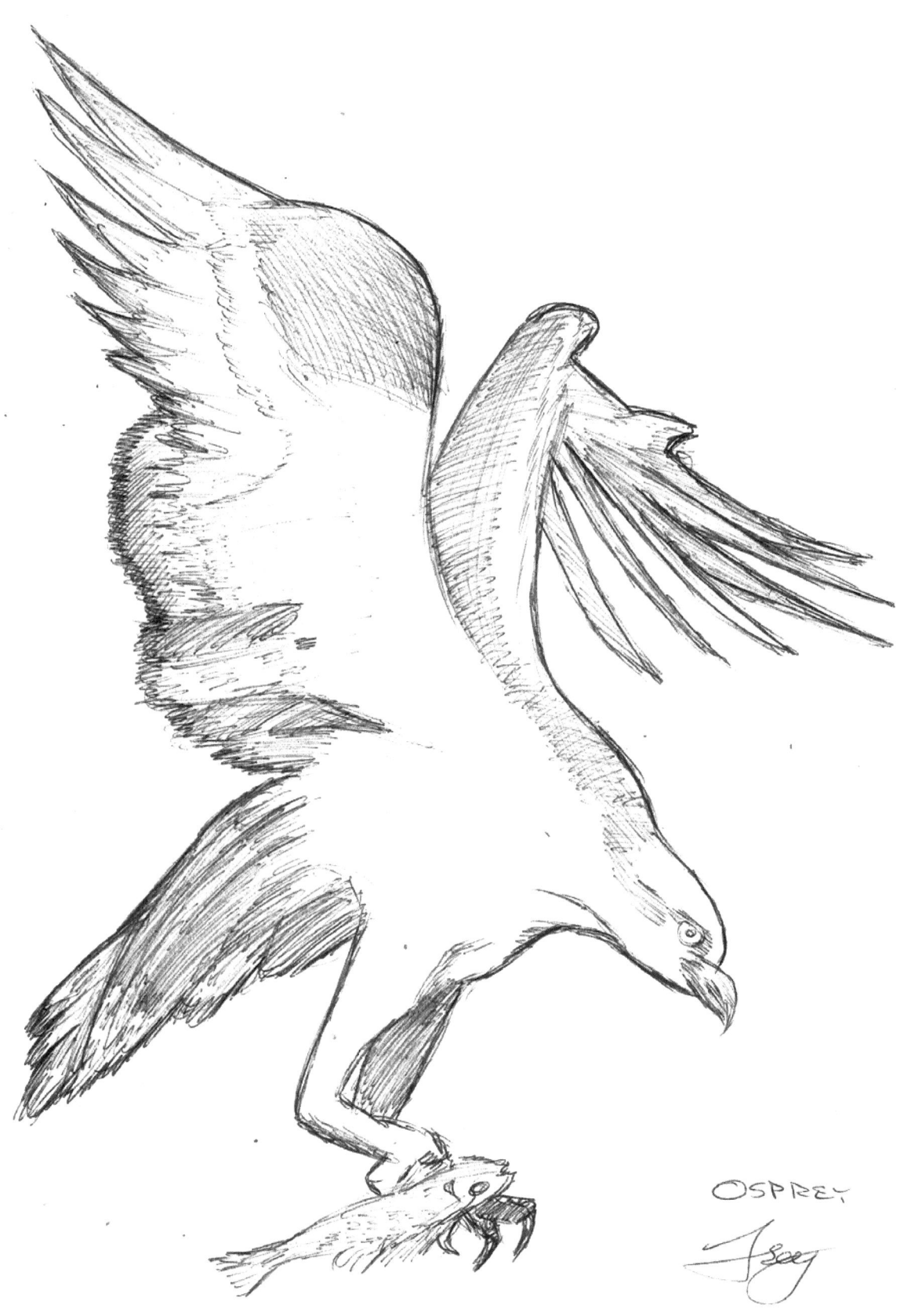

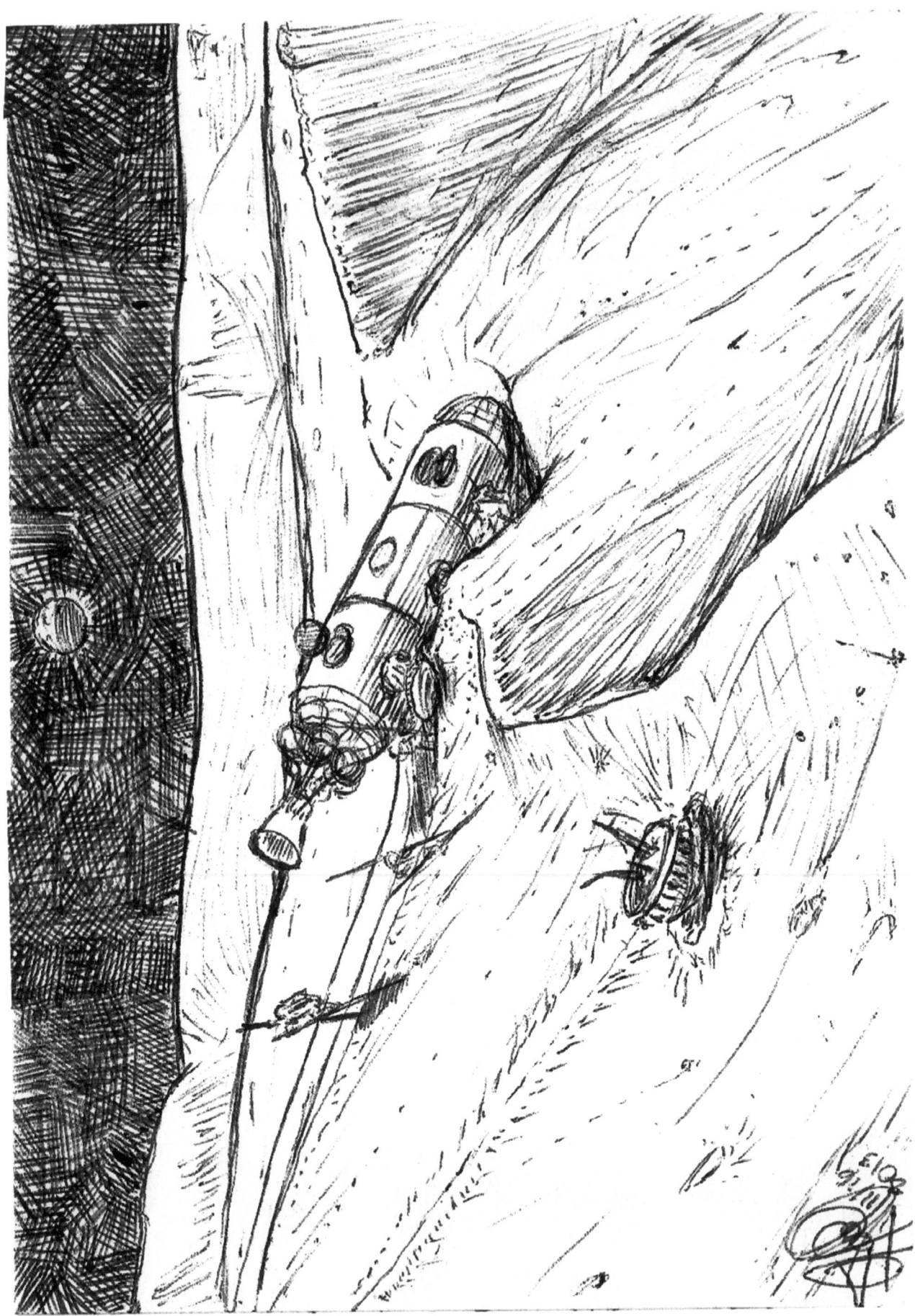

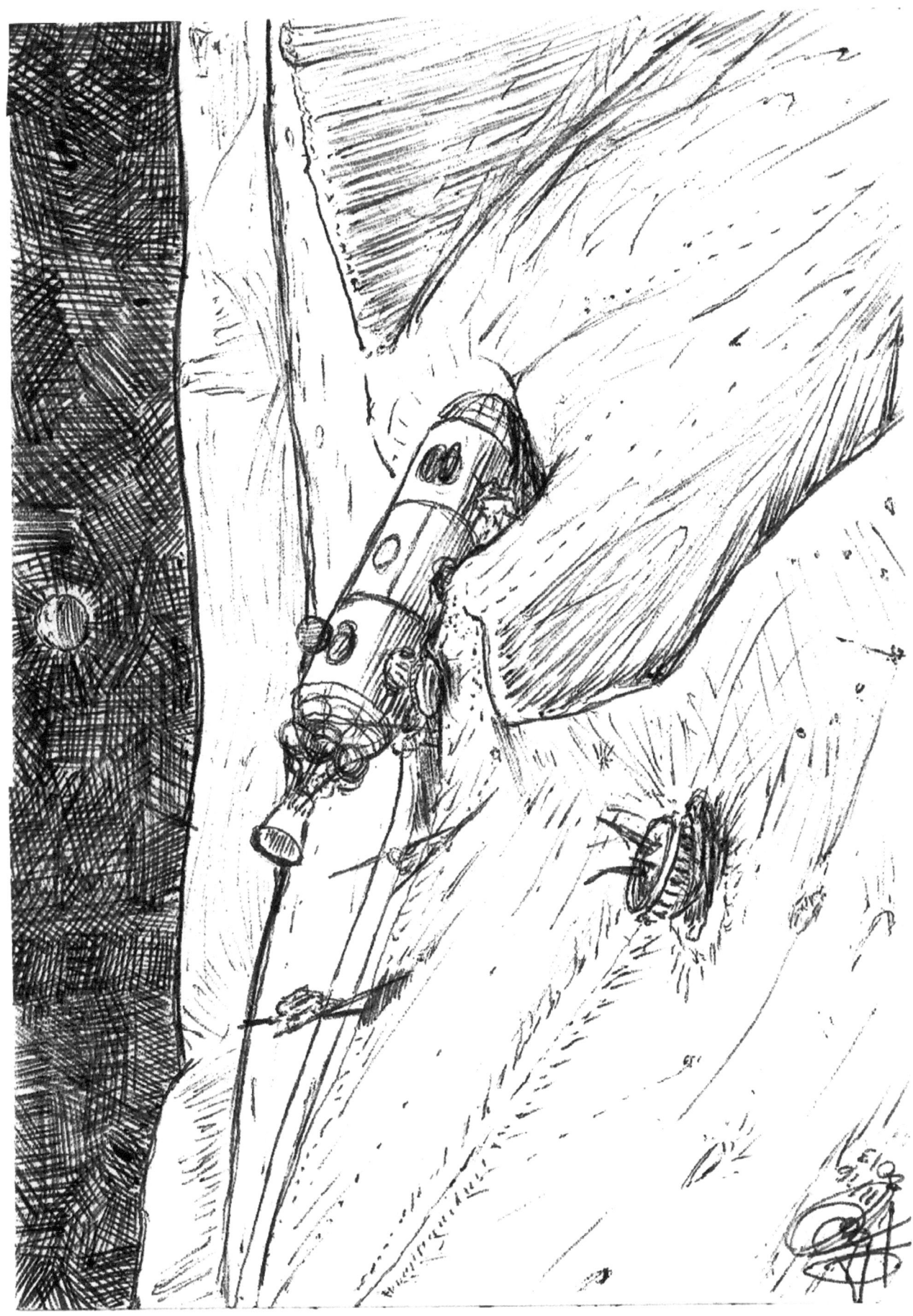

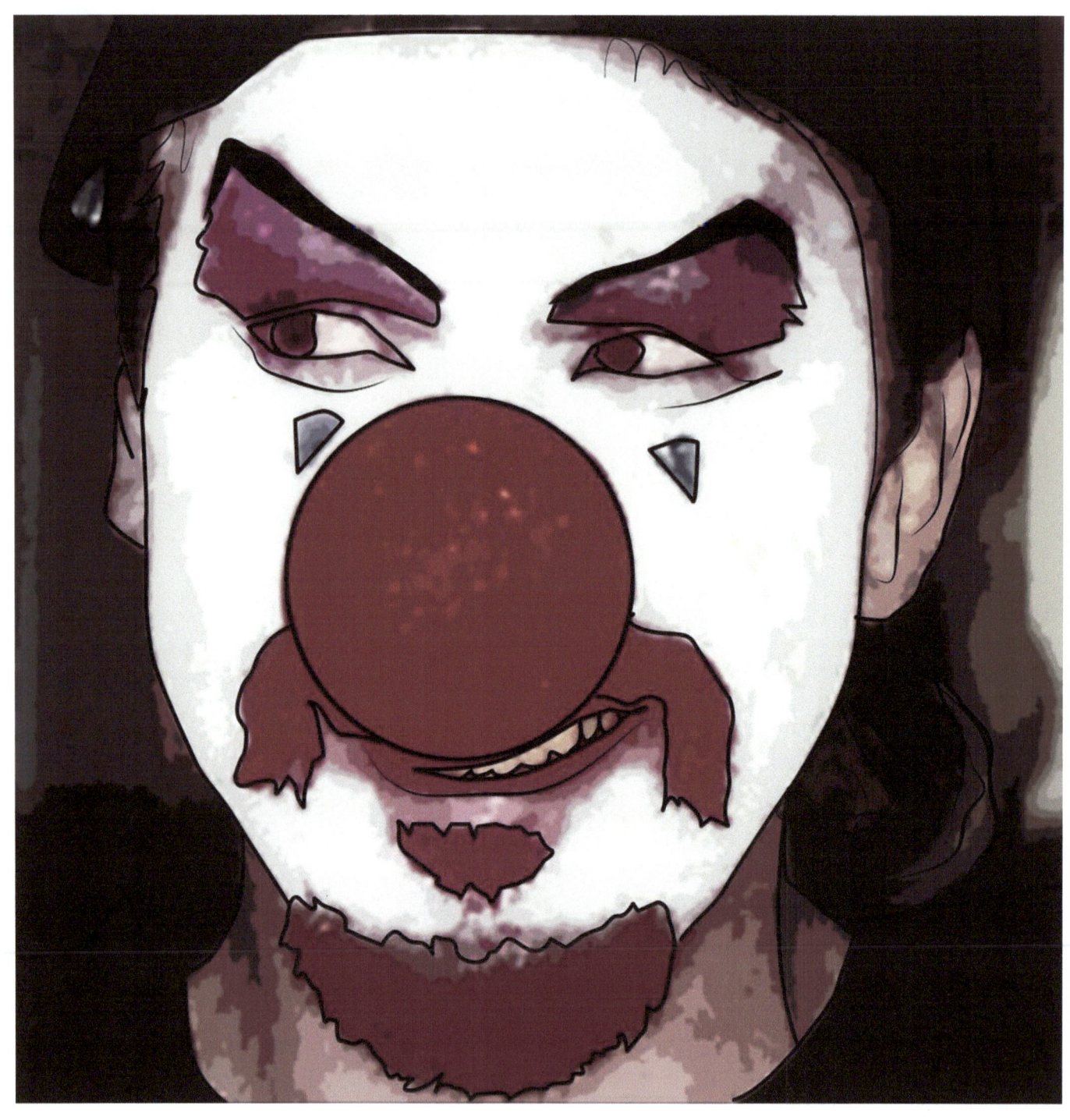

ABOUT THE AUTHOR

James "Trey" Howell lives in penury in southern Virginia. He pretends to write, pretends to be an artist, and right now, he's pretending to work while he tends to his ailing father. Don't cry for him; he'd have changed everything to do what he's doing right now.

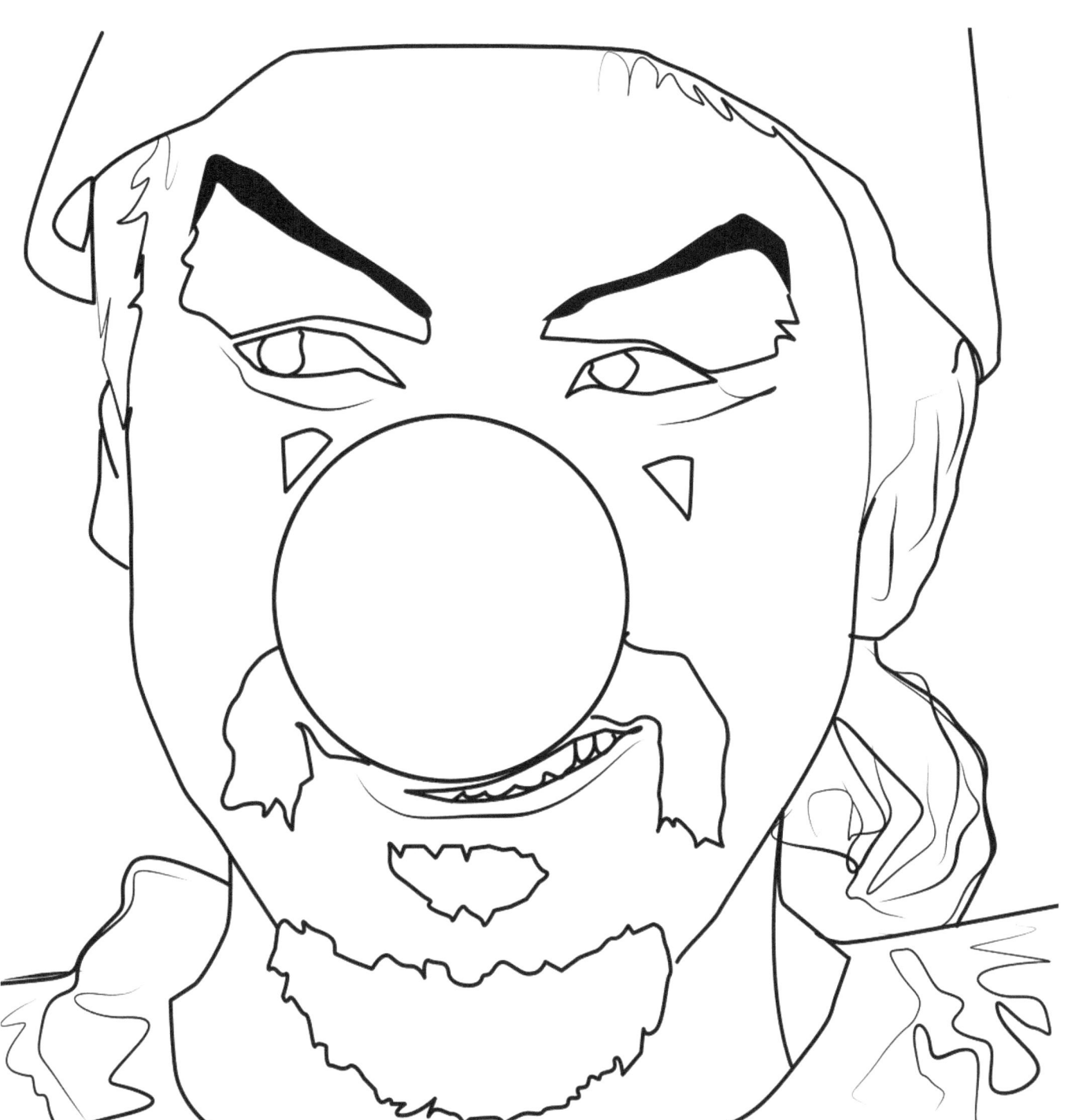

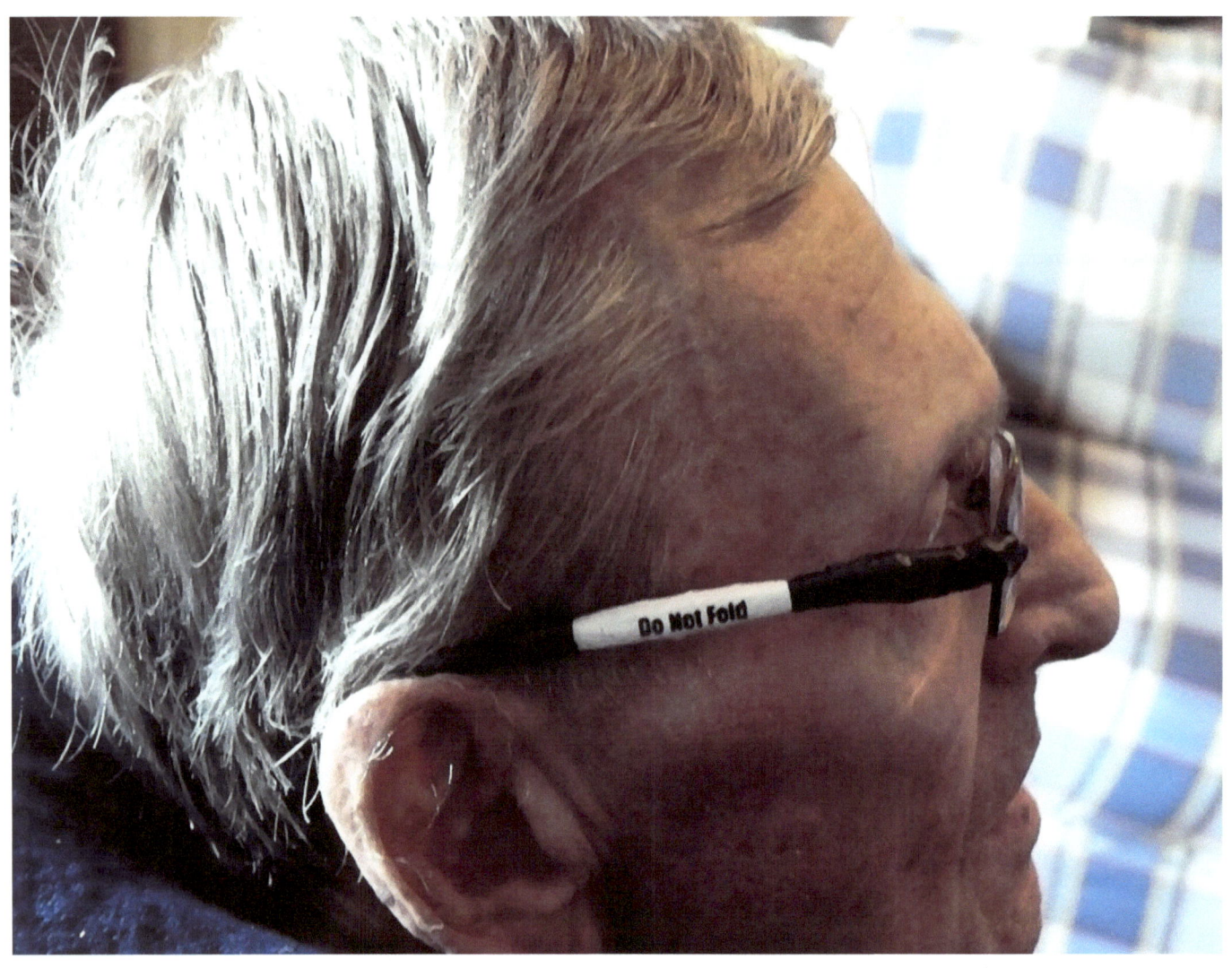

ABOUT THE AUTHOR'S FATHER

"Sonny" Howell is a UVA engineer. He helped design the descent engine of the Lunar Module and worked on the Labeled Release experiment on Viking, which famously sent back positive signs of life from Mars, from both landers on opposite sides of the planet, in 1976. "I didn't build that damned thing so that it could fail," he says whenever the subject comes up. He's rarely wrong.

He's pretty much the greatest dad who ever existed, an explosives and rocketry expert who likes history, tinkering with overpowered cars, and talking about anything a child or adult could ever ask about. He is the author's greatest teacher, and his best friend. "Most of the time I am a sane human being," he said recently, "and then I do something that's stupid as hell." The apple did not fall far from the tree.

www.ingramcontent.com/pod-product-compliance
Lightning Source LLC
Chambersburg PA
CBHW051158220526
45473CB00003B/818